DATE			

THE COMPLETE
RECREATIONAL
VEHICLE COOKBOOK
for Campers, Vans, R.V.'s and Motor Homes

THE COMPLETE
RECREATIONAL
VEHICLE COOKBOOK
for Campers, Vans, R.V.'s and Motor Homes

Gayle and Robert Fletcher Allen

CELESTIAL ARTS
Millbrae, California

For Florence and Reed
who planted the seed.

Copyright © 1977 by Gayle and Robert Fletcher Allen

First printing, February 1977

Made in the United States of America

Library of Congress Cataloging in Publication Data

Allen, Gayle, 1929-
The complete recreational vehicle cookbook for campers, motorhomes, R.V.'s and vans.

1. Cookery. 2. Outdoor cookery. 3. Mobile home living.
I. Allen, Robert Fletcher, 1925-   joint author. II Title.
III. Title: Recreational vehicle cookbook.

TX840.M6A44   641.5'75   76-54176

ISBN 0-89087-174-4

1 2 3 4 5 6 7 8 — 82 81 80 79 78 77

CONTENTS

INTRODUCTION

The idea of outdoor recreation is not new. Mankind has been seeking departures from his regular domicile for centuries. But for the past several decades the use of motorized, outdoor recreational vehicles has so sophisticated the concept there is little resemblance to the earliest forms of outdoor recreation.

Once the outdoor excursion consisted of pitching a canvas tent under the sprawling branches of a tree, perhaps beside a fast-moving brook, cooking haphazardly over an open fire, washing cookware with the abrasive sand of the stream and eating mostly from tins.

A great many changes have taken place. Today, the range of sophisticated motor vehicles for camping in the out-of-doors is enormous. There are fully equipped motor homes so totally self-contained as to leave no reasonable amenity wanting. With their own air conditioning, full bathrooms (often with a tub and shower), hot and cold running water fed from storage tanks, gas-fired water heaters, four burner, propane-fed cooking surfaces and full-sized ovens, electric/gas refrigerators (with separate freezer compartments), eight track stereo tape systems, self-contained electricity generating plants, and sleeping accommodations for up to eight people, these vehicles are truly, as billed, "homes-on-wheels."

1

Of course, all recreational vehicles are not as sophisticated as the motor homes described. The range of appointments step downward to include the most elementary and simplified camper units. There is a unit to suit every taste and every pocketbook and the numbers of these units are growing.

The Complete Recreational Vehicle Cookbook is, as the name implies, a carefully compiled array of the finest recipes selected primarily for their adaptation to cooking in campers, motor homes, RVs, and vans. We have experimented with and developed to a state of personal satisfaction an elaborate chain of exciting recipes which we feel will be enjoyed by most camper enthusiasts. This, after sixty thousand miles of travel in various recreational vehicles of virtually every type available and covering much of this hemisphere, and in every season.

About twenty-five percent of outdoor recreational time is spent in either meal planning or cooking, eating or washing dishes and utensils. Therefore, all of the recipes and techniques in this book have been selected on the basis of ease of preparation, foodstuffs availability, taste acceptance and finally, although certainly not last in importance, nutritional value. We feel that it is inappropriate to neglect this facet of food fare, for it is extremely important to our general health and well-being. In fact, we feel it is poorly advised to alter our general eating habits drastically at any time, particularly during travel. Too many good vacations have been spoiled by stomach upset. It is foolish to sacrifice valuable recreation time because of careless sanitation, overindulgence or anything which might tend to upset our systems. After all, recreational time should be spent in pleasure, *not* having to cope with problems.

One final thought on camper-prepared foods. Camper vacations *should* be designed for the entire family. The fun, as well as the chores, should be for all. Everyone should get into the act. This is as true for a family of two, as for a family of twelve. By involving everyone there are many opportunities for self-expression and a feeling of self-worth.

To dispatch the youngsters into a blackberry bramble is the beginning of a great cobbler for dessert. And, when everyone pitches in to do the dishes, the job gets done and there's a good chance for improved communications between all members of the family. Individual responsibility is an important part of life and here's a good chance to rehearse it.

Whether your camper is among the most sophisticated on the road or the simplest or most modest, good food, thoughtfully prepared with great anticipation and zeal, can very well be remembered as the high point of the entire event. So, experiment when you feel inclined, accept or reject as you will, but most of all enjoy yourself.

GETTING THERE IS HALF THE FUN

We spend more time planning trips in our camper than we actually spend on the road, but the planning has become a highlight of the entire travel adventure attitude in our family. And since we put a great deal of emphasis on the role of food while in the out-of-doors, we spend a great deal of time planning that too.

For example, many winter evenings are spent gathered around our fireplace reminiscing about great experiences on recent or past trips. Those evenings we usually wind up showing movies, slides or photo albums or recounting foods that have gained enough distinction to be talked about again. Sometimes recalling an exotic or particularly delicious dish prepared in the camper will send us scurrying into the kitchen to attempt to duplicate it at home.

A classic example is our "Banana Flambé," one of the simplest dishes imaginable, yet one of the most delicious we've ever conceived. This wonderful recipe was developed out of desperation. On one of our trips to British Columbia, Canada, we ventured off Provincial Route 97 to investigate the rough, backcountry on the route to Bella Coola, a small seaport on the Pacific coast. The tedious rock and gravel road winds about two hundred and fifty miles across a high plateau. We averaged eighteen miles per hour during the day and spent the better part of two days making the trip. We were impressed enough to want to return in spite of the tiresomeness of the hours spent on the bumpy road.

Prior to reaching Bella Coola we discovered the beauty of Tweedsmuir Provincial Park, a majestic mass of lodge-pole pines, valleys and streams. We were so taken by the splendor of the area that we decided to spend a week more than we had planned.

There is also Nimpo Lake and Anahim Lake where we found the fishing excellent. Staying in the area longer than we'd planned put some pressure on our food supplies since we'd figured we would restock in a large town after our trip to the interior. Needless to say, the out-of-doors stimulates the appetite and our provisions got lower. Part of the problem was solved by the fact that we caught goodly numbers of lake trout each day and their delicious taste is satisfying for days on end. The constant request was for desserts and our sugar supplies were very low as well as other items of dessert nature. We had bought a large number of unripe bananas in Vancouver and decided to build a new dessert using them as the principal ingredient. The result was "Banana Flambé." The recipe is found on page 159.

COOKING IN A CAMPER

Our first efforts at cooking in a camper were unusual. It is possible that the unusual circumstances which surrounded that first trip may have set the stage for later successes.

We have jointly produced industrial motion pictures for a number of years and in 1970 we were asked to translate the convenience and recreational pleasure offered by a motor home manufacturer into the medium of a color/sound film. The manufacturer wanted this film to portray an average vacation of a somewhat typical family in a motor home, which would provoke desire on the part of the viewers to participate in the pleasure by purchasing such a vehicle.

The opportunity to produce this film occurred during the production of another film and we were pressed for time. We accepted the assignment since our own family was well-suited to the presentation. We were to take the vehicle on a somewhat sophisticated itinerary through parts of the Pacific Northwest and western British Columbia, Canada. We were to use a typical motor home from the manufacturer and were given six weeks to complete the trip and assemble the film footage.

Having just finished the other project, we had only a few days to prepare for the trip itself. Most of our time was spent getting filming gear in shape for the production and plotting the itinerary. And then we were off. Soon we realized that we'd spent very little time planning how or what we would eat.

Frankly, this was not the way to begin an extensive trip in a recreational vehicle totally unknown to us, on an itinerary which would take us into an area of the hemisphere not previously traveled, and, perhaps more importantly, with no real experience at food preparation outside the comfort and convenience of our own, familiar kitchen.

We immediately equated ourselves with the early pioneers who wound their way across the plains of the West, but as we discovered the extent to which the designer of the vehicle had gone to ensure success, our attitude changed and with it, the realization that we had every reasonable amenity found in our kitchen at home. There were differences however. Differences which would lead us to change a great many ways of preparing foods, and in planning for the meals in question.

To realize the foregoing after traveling some four hundred miles from home was a bit of a shock, but we were adaptable. In fact we found adaptations of at-home favorites which more than please the palate, more than satisfy needs for nutrition and certainly satisfy the desire to accomplish the act without spending excessive time in preparation.

The filming expedition preempted all other than basic needs, but alas, hunger seeks its own reward and food found its way into an upper priority. Here we were, faced with shooting footage for a travel-oriented sales film, viewing the passing scenery with some appreciation *and* preparing three meals a day in unfamiliar surroundings.

In the years since, we have traveled many thousands of miles by such means and have seen the principal sights this hemisphere has to offer and simultaneously enjoyed an adapted cuisine which almost makes us more discontent at home than on the go.

Moreover, we are reminded that we are not alone. There are millions of travel enthusiasts who have been captivated by this mode of travel. The inventory of travel type camping vehicles has reached an astounding figure. Travel-hungry millions are able to alter their lifestyles in a variety of ways and so satisfactorily as to cause millions of others to try it.

Cooking in the camper can be fun, filling and satisfying. Here's the way to do it.

YOUR CAMPER

The range of types of recreational camping vehicles is enormous. As a camper owner you've probably seen virtually every type produced since your interest was stimulated. At some point you decided which was right for you and your family. Regardless of the type you own or use, you have either discovered, or are on the road to discovering, many of the best uses of the vehicle for family fun and relaxation. Also, you have probably developed a number of systems and techniques to prepare and serve food.

If your vehicle is large enough and equipped with an oven, you are able to prepare more foods than range top varieties. If your unit has a refrigerator with a freezer section, you are able to accomplish more than without them. If you have a double sink and holding tank for waste water, your dishwashing and cleanup chores will be easier, but certainly no-less satisfactory.

The simple fact is, regardless of how simple or how elaborate the food preparation facilities may be, the secret of success is how you go about it.

Our objective in *The Complete Recreational Vehicle Cookbook* is to share a variety of tasty, satisfying dishes, together with preparation techniques while on the go. Some will be the simplest imaginable, others more complex and demanding, but each will have the basic elements we all desire: taste, nutrition and ease of preparation in your camper.

We have seen campers which are paraphernalia poor, with too many pieces of cooking equipment and not enough attention given to the idea that cooking on the go should be fun as well as stimulating to the appetite. It is entirely possible to prepare a great many dishes without extraordinary equipment.

The recipes in this book are adaptable to your vehicle regardless of type, size or sophistication.

THE CAMPER GALLEY

How you cook is more important than where and on what kind of equipment. Our kitchens at home are usually planned for efficiency. The galley of the camper has received a great deal of attention in its design to accomplish the same result. For most of us, however, the transition can be awkward because it is smaller and has fewer of the "at home" appointments.

Many campers now boast full-sized or slightly smaller ovens in addition to the countertop cooking surfaces. If your vehicle is so equipped, the extent of your camper "cuisine" is broadened. If not, there is no need to feel intimidated since there are many inventive ways to duplicate the advantages.

Some smaller campers have two burner, propane or butane counter cooking units. Others have three and four burners. The trick is to plan for efficiency while preparing meals. Many things can be primarily cooked in advance, making a burner available for dishes requiring an immediate heat source. Later, and just prior to serving time, the previously cooked dish may be effectively reheated, or, as is our practice for elaborate meals or for larger numbers of people, kept hot on an auxiliary surface. Many times we will start a small fire in an outdoor campground stove, simply to use as a "holding area" for foods already cooked. Most experienced campers today have learned to be inventive in this regard.

The galley is the cook's domain and too many cooks *can* "spoil the broth." As a matter of fact, they can ruin it. Decide who will be cooking at a particular mealtime and keep it that way!

IF YOU DON'T HAVE AN OVEN

Some campers are not equipped with an oven but there are numerous ways to overcome this. The following improvisations have certain frailties but with a bit of invention, patience and a desire to achieve, the problem is solved.

1) Stove top ovens of various sizes and appointments are available at camper and motor home supply outlets. Some of these units have temperature gauges and this can take the guesswork out of cooking temperatures. Others are extremely simple, but nevertheless effective.

2) A simple oven may be created by fastening two aluminum pie pans together with clothes pins, paper clips or other fastening devices. A hole should be punched in the center of each pie pan to release steam build-up.

3) An old deep-well cooker pot or other deep pot can serve as a stove top oven by putting a small amount of water in the bottom and a small trivet on which to set the baking utensil. Be sure to replace the water as it cooks away. Baked potatoes cooked by this means are exceptional, because the moisture from the water at the heat source tends to semisteam them.

4) A reflector type oven can be used at a campfire or at the stove top unit. This is generally a bit slower since much of the heat source dissipates, but it is very satisfactory.

5) Carefully experimenting, you can discover other oven substitutes using aluminum foil hoods or encasements for cooking pots.

6) A dutch oven or pressure cooker with a well-fitting lid can may be used with good results.

REFRIGERATION

The cookstove is but one-half of the galley team. The refrigeration or food preserving section is of equal importance. The perishability of most foods demands that they be properly cared for lest they spoil and be rendered useless. This is not only inconvenient and potentially dangerous to our digestive systems, but also expensive.

If your camper is equipped with a larger model refrigerator and has a freezer section as well, your camper cuisine will have greater latitude. Since we've traveled with everything from an ice chest to the freezer-equipped refrigerator, we've developed techniques adaptable to each model.

The type and size of your cooling compartment will greatly control the amount and variety of foods to be kept cool on the go. Obviously, the larger the unit, the more versatility.

Many campers today have "three-way" refrigerator systems, that is, a combination of gas, 110 volt AC, or 12 volt DC power sources. Gas operated models are generally efficient but oftentimes the "pilot" flame is extinguished by drafts in transit or when the vehicle is not suitably level when parked. This can be a nuisance. It can also be wasteful if food spoils because of lack of cooling.

Naturally the 110 volt AC systems are the best, but require a hookup for the power supply and most of us prefer camping in as remote a location as we can find.

A 12 volt DC system using one or more "deep-cycle" storage batteries can be very efficient and satisfactory for very short periods (usually twelve to eighteen hours between charging) but this can be a gross interference, particularly on the occasions when we want to stay put for several days.

Understanding your own refrigeration system is very important, for if you know how long it will provide good cooling and under what circumstances, a great many disappointments can be avoided.

There are several general rules which control the efficiency of camper refrigeration systems:

1) Keep cooling settings as low as possible to ensure proper cooling temperatures for foods.

2) Cool only food items which require it.

3) Open and close the refrigerator as little as possible. Plan to replace or remove food items to be used at the same opening or closing.

4) If the refrigerator is a gas model, be certain to "level" the camper immediately upon arrival at the site. Check the pilot often to determine if the unit is operating properly.

5) If your camper is equipped with a 12 volt DC system, allow the engine to idle frequently to recharge the batteries. As a reminder to those of us who might forget that peace and quiet are two of the important reasons we venture into the outdoors in the first place we suggest that the engine be run only during daylight hours so as to keep the noise in the campground to a minimum.

6) Check the system frequently to make sure things are in good operating order.

7) Chill or cool many food items in tightly closed containers at the water's edge of a nearby stream to conserve the valuable space of the camper refrigerator.

COOKING UTENSILS FOR THE CAMPER

The cooking utensils used in your camper are not necessarily the same as those used in the kitchen at home. Our general rule is to outfit the camper with everything we will need, yet restrained enough for convenient storage.

For example: We all usually have from four to six saucepans of various sizes in our "at home" kitchen. We have only two in our camper. One holds two quarts, the other about a pint. We figure that's all we need. We have two skillets; one a medium-sized cast iron, the other is a larger, Teflon-coated model. All are hand-downs from our kitchen at home and the sizes have satisfied every need in thousands of miles of camper and motor home travel.

The following lists of utensils and other cooking equipment should be adequate. List A is a basic list. List B is more elaborate for larger vehicles with more storage space or for longer trips.

A	B
2 quart saucepan	1 quart saucepan
1 pint saucepan	
1 six-inch cast iron skillet	1 ten-inch cast iron skillet
1 ten-inch Teflon-coated skillet	
1 eight-cup coffee maker	
2 long-handled forks	
1 spatula	1 bacon turner (tongs)
1 can opener	
1 bottle opener	1 corkscrew
1 paring knife	
1 butcher-type knife	1 egg beater
1 egg turner	
1 vegetable peeler	kitchen shears
1 wire whisk	
plastic glasses	2 quart casserole
nested plastic bowls	pressure cooker
wooden salad bowls	nine-inch pie pan
muffin tin	dutch oven
plastic juice pitcher	1 cake pan
1 stainless steel bowl	habachi
cookie sheet	
measuring cups	long-handled popcorn popper
measuring spoons	
2 large serving spoons	
knife sharpener	

sectioned serving plates

cups and mugs

4 potholders

stainless silverware

grater

plastic flatware

outdoor grill

Toast Tight (description on page 158)

Also:

plastic glassware
wooden spoons
plastic margarine cups with tops
empty coffee cans with tops
jelly jars with tops
aluminum foil
plastic wrap
paper plates
paper cups
paper shopping bags
plastic garbage bags
paper towels
paper napkins
wooden matches
biodegradeable detergent for dishwashing
dish towels
scouring pads
cleanser

And perhaps: A campstove for outdoor cooking. Propane, or standard fuel models are very handy. Also, sterno for emergencies.

Find tricky places, out of the way yet easily accessible, for storing these items. Disposable items shorten the work time for preparaton and cleanup.

PLANNING FOR NUTRITION

The fact that we require large amounts of vitamins and minerals daily should not be overlooked on camper excursions. As a matter of fact, the increased amount of exercise alone will put greater demands on our bodies. so nutrition becomes increasingly important.

The fresher, more wholesome food we eat, the more responsive our bodies are to heavy activity demands. We make a practice of supplementing our daily diets at home with vitamins and selected minerals and continue that regime in the out-of-doors too.

Whole-grained breads, fresh vegetables, fresh and ripe fruits and lots of liquid are all important to our health regardless of where we may be. This is not the time to neglect those needs.

We keep on the lookout for these fresh commodities as we travel. If corn is being harvested nearby, we arrange to buy some from a local farmer or produce stand. Fresh fruits and vegetables are available almost everywhere today. Since many of these items are highly perishable when ripe, plan to eat those first and then rely on canned or otherwise preserved foods.

The other elements of health, exercise, sleep and contentment seem to fall into place all on their own. Sleeplessness is a rarity in the outdoors. Exercise happens quite naturally. Contented spirit is a natural outgrowth of the entire event, so really the only facet to be given much attention *is* nutrition.

OUR ENVIRONMENT

Some of the endless abuses perpetrated against our environment are now beginning to show. Many of our streams are so polluted they are unfit for use of any kind. Some are so sight-polluted they make many of us shake our heads in despair.

Years ago the problem was scarcely noticeable. Oh, you might see an occasional tin can or bit of paper but the can soon rusted away and the paper dissolved into the soil and was forgotten. A number of things have changed.

Population increases have conbined with new and less fragile food containers, along with expanded numbers fleeing the cities to the clear air of the outdoors, and have begun to cause serious problems. The problems of pollution have been talked about, legislated against and coped with on various levels, but the simple fact is, not much has happened to reduce the careless abandon with which litter, waste and pollutants scar our landscapes.

It was either a politician running for office or a campground philosopher who stated, "One day we'll all stand knee-deep in soft drink can pull tabs and wonder how we'll ever dig our way out."

Perhaps that overstates the problem, but it sure makes you think. Are we destroying the very beauty we strain to get to on a busy weekend? Is the litter problem and pollution situation of genuine concern? We think it should be considered.

No one since the dawn of human history ever wanted to stand alone on any issue, but we all know that men have done just that. We don't want to stand alone or with few and scattered allies on the matter of litter and pollution. No, we'd much prefer that many people—most people—would think seriously before discarding plastic, paper, aluminum, glass, tin, and assorted litter over square miles of campgrounds intended to be enjoyed rather than defaced. So, one thing is clear. If we stand any chance of having uncluttered camping facilities in our future, or our children's future, or their children's future, care will have to be taken.

Some guides:

1) Use refuse containers for *all* noncombustible refuse.

2) Burn all burnable refuse.

3) Be careful with cans, bottles, paper, plastic and anything which is not promptly discarded.

4) Regardless of how distasteful the task, clean up debris when *you* find it. (It's easier to do if you stop to realize that you already pick up after others in a variety of less graphic ways—i.e., taxes, etc.)

5) Use biodegradeable detergents for dishwashing and the like. Never dump anything into a lake or stream. Never clean fish in a lake or stream.

6) Instruct everyone in your family or group to obey these simple rules, if only for the sake of decency.

CAMPER COOKING SAFETY

It is as appropriate to be careful and prepared for cooking accidents in the camper as it is at home, and since the camper has less space and fewer safety devices than the home kitchen, there are a variety of precautions which may solve many problems. There is no need for a vacation to be spoiled by an accident that may cause pain and injury to any family member. There are a number of pertinent rules used in our camper.

1) Although help at the cooking surface may be appreciated, we generally allow only one person there at a time. Hot utensils and their contents can cause serious burns if a mishap results from too many bodies at the wrong time.

2) A working fire extinguisher is kept within reach of the cooking area at all times. Ours is positioned in such a way

that it is readily available regardless of where a fire might occur. There is no merit in having the extinguisher beyond the reach of someone at the site of a grease fire. Our extinguisher is part of a pretrip check list. Its capacity to be in working order is checked by a gauge.

3) We all cautiously use the cooking area with the idea that a fire can not only ruin the food in preparation, but possibly result in a serious personal injury. We try not to approach the problem with fear, but rather with monitored good judgment.

4) We have a rather elaborate first-aid kit at hand at all times. Even the simplest burn should have prompt attention.

We also have a good paperback volume on first-aid treatment in the camper. There is nothing worse than to sustain an injury and not know how to properly render emergency treatment.

5) Regardless of the circumstances, we plan never to be in a hurry about cooking anything. Frenzied cooking usually ends in a disaster of some kind.

6) Sharp tools of any kind are used only by those qualified.

7) Combustible materials are *never* allowed in the cooking area.

8) If there is *any* suspicion of spoilage, the food in question is discarded promptly. Nobody wants to be sick on holiday!

9) One further general health plan is religiously followed. If we plan to spend several days in a campground we get the name, address and telephone number of a local doctor of medicine from the telephone directory of the town nearest the campground or camping area. Fortunately we've never

needed to use the information, but it is comforting to have in the event of an emergency.

10) Make every effort to get your vehicle as level as possible. The cooking surface of your unit should be as level as possible because cooking pots and skillets tend to slide otherwise, which is dangerous.

11) At serving time, warn everyone about hot plates, bowls and cups. The surprise discovery that a metal plate is very hot can cause its contents to be flung in various directions.

SEASONING WITH HERBS AND SPICES

It is a little disconcerting to realize that the practice of seasoning foods with herbs and spices began in the Old World in order to mask the odor and taste of bad food. Most of us now use these flavor enhancers to broaden the flavors of various foods. We all take along salt and pepper on our camping excursions, so why not take along a few herbs and selected spices?

We believe duplicating the at-home herb and spice inventory is taking the matter a bit too far, but there are a number that we find worthwhile to take in the camper.

If you are a seasonal camper only, you will want to take only very small supplies because the volatile oils are lost after exposure to heat and light. If you camp year-round, and spices are used and replaced regularly, they can be kept in the camper as a permanent cabinet item. We consider the following essential:

salt	parsley (dried)
pepper	paprika
garlic salt	*Spike
onion salt	monosodium glutamate

*Spike is a commercial seasoning which we find indispensable at home or away. It contains salt, saffron, Indian curry, papaya, white pepper, horseradish, oregano, tarragon, sage, basil, summer savory, green and red peppers, parsley, sea greens, dill, toasted onion, yeast concentrate, orange and lemon peel, dextrose, mushrooms, rosehips, celery root, tomato and watercress.

This seasoning is so versatile that if we were restricted to any three seasonings we would take along salt, pepper and Spike. The only source we know of for this delightful cooking amenity is in health food stores.

Optional herbs and spices:

vanilla	chili powder
cinnamon	bay leaves
nutmeg	basil
oregano	dill weed
dry mustard	seasoned salt
curry powder	seasoned pepper

If you plan on soups and stews on your outings take along bouquet garni which you can make up at home before the trip. For each you will need:

1 four-inch square cheesecloth
2 small sprigs fresh parsley
2 small sprigs thyme
1 bay leaf

Tie herbs up in the cheesecloth and secure with a bit of string. If you don't have fresh herbs, substitute one teaspoon each of the parsley and thyme. Store in small foil packets or airtight can.

Careful experimentation can very often turn good food into really great food using these seasonings.

A SMATTERING OF SNACK FOODS

Traveling seems to increase the craving for something to snack on. This occurs at the usual snack hours and also at some really out of the ordinary times.

Once, at two o'clock in the morning after viewing the "northern lights" we simply had to have something to snack on while talking over this remarkable experience. Fortunately, it was not our first trip out so we were prepared. We feel the snacks should be as nourishing as possible. We have lots of packaged favorites and also some "do-ahead" and "take-alongs."

Things to Have on Hand

sesame crackers
wheat thins
soda crackers
peanut butter
corn chips
nuts and bolts—recipe given
    on page 31
canned pineapple chunks
flour tortillas
corn tortillas
salsa (sauce)
cheese—both bulk and
    spreadables

chopped green chilies
refrigerator biscuits and rolls
prepared biscuit mix—
    purchased or your own
Vienna sausages
sour cream
dry soup mixes—onion and
    beef mushroom
prepared piecrust mix
sausage
bacon
Parmesan cheese
popcorn

The following recipes are interchangeable as snack foods and hors d'oeuvres. Many is the time we've made a full meal from several snack foods served at once. We call it simply, an hors d'oeuvre dinner. It is marvelous at sporting events scheduled during mealtime.

Sizzling Pineapple

For each person you will need four or five, depending on appetites.

> pineapple chunks—canned or fresh
> strips of bacon—cut in half

These are delicious cooked over a bed of hot coals. A sterno can may be substituted for the heat source. You may lay them on a grill and turn with tongs or let everyone cook their own on a bamboo skewer or stick.

Wrap a half strip of bacon around a pineapple chunk and secure with a toothpick if cooking over coals. If using a skewer, use it to fasten the bacon. Cook until the bacon is crisp and brown. Turn to prevent burning. The juice of the pineapple drips through and the aroma is magnificent. We seem to have trouble cooking enough to serve on a platter; they are usually eaten as fast as they are cooked.

Pink Crackers

soda crackers   paprika
butter—softened   baking sheet

Spread soda crackers with soft butter. Sprinkle generously with paprika. Run under the broiler until crackers are lightly browned and bubbly. Serve at once.

Cheese Crispies

These can be prepared early in the day and finished at serving time or totally prepared at the last minute. We like them chilled so if we think of it in time, we prepare them early in the day. Excluding the driver, we've even made them while riding along in a thunderstorm. Our favorite spread is pimento with bacon.

flavored cheese spread—jars or cartons
crushed corn chips

Grease the palms of your hands and form small bite-size balls of the cheese spread. Use several different kinds if you wish. Store in the refrigerator until ready to serve. At serving time crush the corn chips. Roll each cheese ball in the crushed chips and arrange on a serving plate (paper plates mean no cleanup).

Spicy Beef Pinwheels

2 packages spicy beef sandwich meat
(about 8 to 10 very thin slices in a package)
1 8 oz. package cream cheese—softened
1 teaspoon grated onion

Lay the thin slices of beef out singly. Mix the cream cheese and grated onion together. Spread a thin layer on each slice of spicy beef and stack three slices thick. Roll each stack into a tight roll similar to a jelly roll. Chill thoroughly. Cut into ¼ inch pinwheels and serve. These are as tasty as they are attractive. Be sure to chill them before trying to slice them. Also freezing before slicing is excellent. The rolls keep for weeks in the freezer.

23

Our Choice Platter

There is nothing like a fresh vegetable platter. So healthy, crunchy and delicious. Prepare a platter of your favorite vegetables, cut into finger handling size. Salt and pepper to taste and serve with a dressing or dip.

green onions	**cucumber sticks**
cherry tomatoes	**sliced raw mushrooms**
zucchini sticks	**sliced raw turnip**
celery sticks	**cauliflower buds**
carrot sticks	**blue cheese dressing or dip**

Wash and prepare all vegetables ahead of time and chill. Arrange on a platter. Put dip in the center or pour over all. We prefer to dip as each of us likes the dip on our vegetables in different amounts.

Blue Cheese Dip
(makes 1 to 1½ cups)

½ cup mayonnaise	**3 tablespoons crumbled blue**
½ cup buttermilk	**cheese**
¼ to ½ cup sour cream	**salt and pepper to taste**
	1 teaspoon chopped
	parsley—optional

Mix all ingredients together and blend well. If you do not wish to make your own dressing, there are good commercial ones available everywhere.

Cucumber Crackers

I personally have adored these little jewels for years and years. Bob and the children would not even venture a taste, but with the passage of time they have learned the error of their ways. One night as I was savoring each bite, I was surprised to hear someone ask to try a taste. Now, after all the years of abstaining, my family is making up for it. Now they consume *more* than their share.

**soda crackers or sesame crackers
sliced cucumbers
homemade mayonnaise
salt and pepper or Spike**

Slice the cucumbers very thin. If they are the hothouse variety you need not peel them. Spread each cracker with a bit of mayonnaise and lay a cucumber slice on top. Season with either salt and pepper or Spike. Spike can be found in health food stores. Make them as you eat them, not a plateful at a time as they will become soggy.

Salami and Swiss

Quick and easy, this could even be a luncheon substitute.

**thin slices of salami
a rectangle slice of Swiss cheese ¼ inch thick
a rectangle slice of dill pickle**

Lay the salami out and place a slice of Swiss cheese and a slice of dill pickle on each. Roll up and lay fold side down or secure with a toothpick. Chill one- half hour before serving. A bowl of mustard to dip as desired.

Prosciutto and Cantaloupe

This authentic Italian hors d'oeuvre is served in fine restaurants around the world. It is a favorite of our on-the-go menus and at home. If you cannot find prosciutto, substitute thinly sliced baked or smoked ham. Slice a fresh cantaloupe into bite-size wedges removing the rind. Wrap prosciutto around the cantaloupe wedges and secure with toothpicks.

Vegetable Kabobs

Something a little different. Served with a steak, hamburger patty or other main dish it makes a very innovative vegetable addition. The following recipe serves four people. Add or subtract for the number you wish to serve.

2 green peppers	¾ cup salad oil
8 small white onions	¼ cup lemon juice
2 firm tomatoes	1 teaspoon sugar
8 large mushrooms	½ teaspoon oregano
salt and pepper to taste	¼ teaspoon chili seasoning

Remove seeds and cut green peppers into eight pieces. If onions are fresh, boil for ten minutes. If canned, use as is. Peel and cut tomatoes into eight quarters. Wash mushrooms and remove stems. Save stems for soup or chop for salads or omelets. Put cut vegetables into a bowl and sprinkle with salt and pepper. Beat salad oil, lemon juice, sugar, oregano and chili seasoning until slightly thickened. Pour over vegetables. Thread on skewers in the order listed until two of each ingredient is on each skewer. Broil in the oven or place on a grill over a charcoal fire or hot coals. Cooking time should be approximately five minutes on each side.

You can do this at the last minute or marinate all day while driving. Flavor does improve with standing.

Parmesan Popcorn

This is an excellent snack food and also an absolutely smashing addition to soups. Serve as a crouton substitute and receive raves.

popped corn
melted butter
Parmesan cheese—packaged or fresh-grated

Pop corn and add as much melted butter as you wish. If you are watching calories, omit the butter. Add Parmesan to generously coat the popcorn. Toss. Serve cold or heat for soups. Also a children-pleaser for salads.

Sweet and Sour

You can use meatballs, cut-up hot dogs, Vienna sausages or cocktail sausages. Our favorites are meatballs and hot dogs. You can prepare as much sauce as needed. This is made by special request for our Christmas open house parties.

meatballs
grape jelly
chili sauce

Make meatballs in bite-size proportions. If using hot dogs, Vienna sausages or cocktail sausages, cut into bite-size pieces. Place in dish and use forks or toothpicks to dip. Put equal parts of grape jelly and chili into a saucepan. Heat until mixture begins to bubble. Stir as needed to blend well. Keep warm while serving. Leftovers will heat up again. Keeps well several days in the refrigerator.

Hot Tortilla Dip

1 lb. cheddar cheese
½ cup milk

1 large can green chili
salsa (sauce)
tortilla chips

Heat cheese and milk in a saucepan over low heat. Stir while melting cheese and blend well. Add salsa. Serve warm. Dip chips in the hot cheese mixture.

Variation: If you do not have enough cheese or you want to cut down on the cost, substitute two cans of cheese soup for the pound of cheese. Add only enough milk to make desired consistency.

Cheese Pinwheels

Serve also with soup and salad in place of sandwiches. Freezes well. May be frozen before or after slicing, whichever is most convenient.

1 recipe piecrust
½ lb. grated cheese—cheddar or Swiss
1 teaspoon onion salt

Prepare piecrust and roll thin. Spread the grated cheese over the entire surface evenly. Sprinkle with onion salt. Roll up jelly roll fashion and press edges together. Chill at least thirty minutes. Slice one-fourth inch thick. Lay on a baking sheet about one inch apart and bake ten to twelve minutes in a 350° oven. Serve warm. Leftovers are good as is even without reheating.

Onion Sticks

Be sure to make extras to use as croutons. Just cut the leftovers into ¼ inch cubes and store in airtight container. They enhance the flavor of salads and soups.

1 cup butter or margarine
1 package dehydrated onion soup mix
15 to 20 slices bread—white or wheat

Mix butter and soup mix together until well blended. Trim crusts from the bread (save for ducks or birds). Spread each slice with butter mixture. Cut each slice into thirds. Lay the strips close together on a baking sheet and bake in a 375° oven seven to eight minutes until slices are browned and crisp.

Sausage Balls

Make ahead or at serving time. At breakfast cook the sausage. Let someone else mix and form the balls while you are doing the breakfast cleanup.

1 lb. sausage—hot or mild
3 cups biscuit mix

10 oz. grated sharp
cheddar cheese
½ teaspoon seasoned salt

Prepare biscuit mix according to directions on box. Mix all ingredients together. Using your hands will make the job easier. Shape into approximately 1″ balls. Bake on a baking sheet in a 375° oven twelve to fifteen minutes until puffed and golden brown.

These are a great variation with eggs at breakfast.

Unusual Snack Spread

The unusual ingredients used in this most appealing spread do not sound as if they would go together at all. We'd advise you to taste it first before reading the ingredients but that's sort of impossible at this point. Best spread on wheat thins or toast rounds.

1 cup crunchy peanut butter
1 cup chili sauce
½ lb. crisp-cooked bacon—crumbled

Mix peanut butter and chili sauce together until well blended. Add the crumbled bacon at the last minute before serving. Spread generously on crackers. Use as a sandwich spread if you have any left over.

Cold Artichokes

Two are usually enough to satisfy four people when served as an appetizer.

2 artichokes
½ cup mayonnaise

¼ cup sour cream
¼ teaspoon curry powder
¼ teaspoon seasoned pepper

Prepare artichokes. Cut off sharp tips and cook in pressure cooker on fifteen pounds pressure exactly fifteen minutes after top jiggles. If you do not have a pressure cooker, cook slowly in boiling salted water forty-five minutes to one hour until tender. Remove at once, run under cold water and chill at least two hours. Mix mayonnaise, sour cream, curry powder and seasoned pepper together. Peel and dip. Makes an attractive tray at a party—at home too.

First Five Days

So-called because we always start out with this snack. We also replenish it during our travels and it always seems to last five days. Provides good nutrition as well as taste enjoyment.

1 package carrots	¼ teaspoon garlic salt
1 bunch celery	5 to 6 ice cubes
¼ teaspoon seasoned salt	1 8″ square cake pan with cover

Wash and scrape carrots. Wash and string celery. Cut into thin sticks and pack rather tightly into the cake pan, sprinkling seasoning on each layer. Put ice cubes around the top and cover. If you do not have a pan with a cover, use plastic wrap but seal the edges tight. Store in the refrigerator and serve as needed.

Cheese Tempters
(makes 3 dozen)

This is a specialty of our daughter's. She makes them about four times a year. Usually the amount is doubled and we keep them in the freezer—ready to travel. She also makes them on request for her college dorm friends.

6 oz. Wisconsin sharp cheddar cheese	½ cup sifted flour
¼ cup butter	¼ teaspoon salt
	1 cup corn flakes
	paprika

Have cheese and butter at room temperature. Combine until well blended. Add the flour and salt and mix well. Add the corn flakes and mix with hands until the mixture holds together. Pinch off small amounts and roll into balls. Roll the balls in paprika until lightly coated. Place on an ungreased baking sheet about two inches apart. Bake in a 400° oven twelve to fifteen minutes.

Note: If short on paprika or a milder flavor is desired, sprinkle paprika on top of balls on baking sheet instead of rolling to coat.

Nuts and Bolts

A nourishing snack any time anywhere. Store in airtight containers and it keeps for weeks.

½ box Rice Chex	½ lb. pecan halves
½ box Cheerios	½ lb. butter
1 box bite-size Ralstons	1 teaspoon celery salt
½ box stick pretzels	1 teaspoon garlic salt

In a large baking pan (we use an old photographic tray) mix together Rice Chex, Cheerios, Ralstons, pretzels and pecans. Melt the butter and drizzle over all evenly. Mix celery salt and garlic salt together and sprinkle over all evenly. Bake in a 250° oven for two hours. Stir every twenty minutes.

Onion Pecans

A tin of these delicious morsels makes a most welcome treat any time during the year. Use it in place of dessert.

1 quart shelled pecans—halves if possible
1 package dried onion soup mix
¼ cup butter-flavored oil
1 teaspoon salt

Toast pecans in a shallow baking pan (cookie sheet is good) in a 300° oven for twenty-five minutes. Crush soup mix with a rolling pin. Mix with oil and stir into nuts until well blended. Roast another twenty minutes, stirring often. Spread on paper towels to drain. Sprinkle with salt, and cool. Store in airtight containers.

Canadian Consul Dip

Serve with any cracker or chip. Regular potato chips are somewhat hard to dip but the ones with ridges are acceptable. The atmosphere of a government dinner with flags flying is pretty impressive. So whenever we partake of this excellent dip we think of our Canadian friends with fond memories.

½ cup chopped onion	½ cup chopped tomatoes
½ cup chopped black olives	1 teaspoon salt
½ cup chopped green chili peppers	2 tablespoons lemon juice

Mix all together and let stand overnight. Stir to mix well before serving. If too much liquid, drain before serving.

Variation: As a really regal sandwich spread, mix with eight ounces of cream cheese and spread open face on rye bread.

Refrigerator Biscuit Bites

Use either packaged biscuits or rolls. Divide each biscuit in half and wrap around half of a Vienna sausage. Bake six to eight minutes in a 350° oven. Serve with mustard as dip.

Quesadillas

One of the best things from Mexico. Every household has its own special way of preparing them. It is one of the simplest ways of satisfying a hungry person or a hungry crowd.

flour or corn tortillas
jack cheese

green chilies—whole or
chopped
oil or butter for frying

Separate the tortillas and sprinkle a layer of grated cheese on top to within one-half inch of the edge. Lay a green chili in the center or spoon one tablespoon chopped chilies in the center. Fold in half. Fry in just enough oil to cover bottom of skillet. Serve hot.

Variations: Use only tortilla and cheese. Grate cheese on open tortilla. Run in the oven until cheese is melted. Fold in half.

Use chopped green chilies and cheese. Put chilies on tortilla. Cover with cheese. Run under the broiler until cheese is melted and bubbly. Remove, cut into quarters and serve.

Toasted Pumpkin Seeds

In most of rural America pumpkins mature in the late summer and can usually be bought along the backroads for a very small price. There is an unusual recipe for pumpkin on page 00. Be sure to save, clean and thoroughly dry the seeds. If you'd rather not be bothered during the trip, save pumpkin seeds during the preceding fall or winter just for this occasion.

> **1 to 2 cups thoroughly dried pumpkin seeds**
> **a bit of oil, butter or margarine**
> **salt**

Melt the oil or butter in a skillet or cookie sheet and distribute the seeds so as to coat with the hot oil. Either stir-fry in a skillet or bake in the oven until the seeds are well-toasted. Salt, cool a bit and serve. Anyone that doesn't enjoy these just isn't trying!

Banana Chips

The first time we enjoyed these was *not* while camping, but we promptly included them as a campsite "nibbler."

While touring the island of Basse-Terre at Guadeloupe in the eastern Caribbean, we were served this as an afternoon refreshment. The plantain banana is found there in extraordinary quantities. These bananas are much smaller than the usual market banana found at home. These are picked green, peeled, thinly sliced, then quickly deep-fried in hot oil, drained and cooled before munching.

ALONG THE SIDE OF THE ROAD

One of the greatest benefits camper travel has to offer is the unique opportunity to discover. For example, the chances for the younger members of the family to see agricultural America are increased on the go. You certainly don't have to be young to appreciate seeing fields of corn, wheat or truck farming produce. If nothing else, it reminds us all where the food we eat comes from and how it is produced. There are also opportunities to buy farm-fresh produce which we might otherwise never have a chance to experience.

Throughout rural America, excess farm production is offered for sale along the road in small stalls or "fruit stands." This provides a chance to obtain some of the freshest and most delicious foods on the go. We've experienced the opportunities so often, we think it should be included.

On one memorable occasion, as we re-entered the United States in Montana after a month in the Canadian Province of Alberta, we began to see dozens of small stalls along the road selling freshly picked cherries. We finally decided to stop and take a closer look. The two small boys tending the simple roadside stand offered us "samples." Without a doubt these were the most delicious we've ever tasted, before or since. We bought a generous supply and were on our way. Stopping for several days on the shores of a magnificent lake, we enjoyed those cherries with a passion. We even produced six quarts of cherry preserves which were enjoyed later at home after the venture had become only a memory. Although you may not want to spend the time and effort necessary to make jams along the way, you'll nevertheless want to be aware of such opportunities.

The "cherry incident," as we now refer to it, is but one isolated occasion in our travels which speaks to the opportunities for finding unusual foodfare along the way. In season, there are corn, beans, watermelon, cantaloupe, onions, potatoes, avocados, peaches, apples, pears, oranges, grapefruit, figs, artichokes, apricots and other fresh produce. As a matter of fact, under the right circumstances, market shopping can be held to a minimum.

We've learned to be on the lookout for a variety of "free" foods along the way. We've found delightful, fresh mint growing wild along the waterline of mountain streams or country creeks. In Wisconsin in the spring we've enjoyed fresh, wild asparagus. We've also found wild raspberries, blackberries, huckleberries, wild crabapples, bimbleberries and blueberries. Some of the wild vegetables we've found and enjoyed include mustard greens, dandelion greens and kale. It *is* important to know what you are looking for and eating, however, because everything that grows is certainly not edible. Younger members of the family should be cautioned to have permission before eating anything growing wild.

There are other things we've found in the out-of-doors to enhance our menus. Some years ago, while camping on the shore of a clear lake, we found one of those "near-perfect" spots and spent several days there. On the afternoon of the first day we planned a picnic near the water's edge. Two of the boys were idly tossing a ball back and forth and as David missed a catch, the ball rolled into the water. As he went to retrieve it, he suddenly looked up with a very surprised expression. He had found a large duck egg. A few feet away he found another and another.

Our ecology-minded family would never have touched those eggs had they been in a nest, but scattered as they were, it was presumed that they had been laid by ducks uninterested in nesting. This is often the case in camping areas where activity and noise discourage formal setting.

Remembering that a family uncle had been particularly fond of duck eggs for breakfast, we spread out in search of other abandoned eggs. Within a few minutes we found three more. We discovered that the eggs were fresh by lowering them into the water at the lake's edge. Since they sank, we knew they were fresh, since carbon dioxide built up in a bad egg would have caused the egg to float. We calculated that by size comparison with market hen's eggs, we had the equivalent of a dozen and more than enough for several breakfasts. Here's what we had the next morning:

Duck Eggs Supreme

    3 tablespoons butter
    4 duck eggs—beaten until fluffy
    2 tablespoons water—added to beaten eggs
    1 teaspoon salt
    ⅛ teaspoon pepper
    ¼ teaspoon basil
    ¼ teaspoon dried parsley
    ¼ teaspoon monosodium glutamate—optional

Melt butter in a skillet. Combine other ingredients. When skillet is hot, quickly pour in the beaten eggs. Lift and let the uncooked egg mixture run down underneath. Cook until medium firm. Beginning at one side fold the edge up and over to the other side. Suddenly you have a magnificent omelet and absolutely unequaled for flavor.

If you don't find duck eggs on your outing, have the omelet anyway and rejoice that you're in the outdoors.

Variation: Fill the omelet with any variety of fillings listed on page 49.

Green Greens

Through most of the United States there is available one of the finest sources of vitamins and minerals to be found in any vegetable. Mustard grows prolifically almost everywhere, but if touring along the west coast, from Mexico to the Canadian border, mustard greens grow in unique abundance.

The Spanish Conquistadors sowed a swath of mustard seed for more than a thousand miles as a marked trail for their followers. Assisted by the reseeding abilities of the mustard plant, even now, hundreds of years later, mustard greens are growing wild. They are good for you and give you a good feeling for "living off the land."

This is another activity for the entire family. Send everyone out into a field of mustard, instructed to pick only the small, tender leaves. Set a short duration time limit. This will add a bit to the competition. Pick about four times the amount you think you'll need, since they cook down quite a bit.

Soak the greens in cold water with a tablespoon or so of salt. This will make the soil loosen easier and cause any clinging insects to loosen their grip and rise to the top of the water for discarding. When thoroughly washed, put into boiling water with about one teaspoon salt added to it. Keep pushing in the greens until all are covered with the boiling water. Continue cooking until just tender. Drain and serve with Tangy Sauce. Honestly, after a meal of these delicious greens you can imagine the early pioneers as they crossed this great land of ours.

Tangy Sauce

½ cup cider vinegar
juice of ½ lemon
⅛ teaspoon sugar

Mix and pour over greens to individual tastes.

Fruit and Berries by the Road

Several recipes are given for apples, crabapples and blackberries.

When picking berries, make sure you are not on private property. If you are in any doubt whatsoever always ask permission.

Ghost Town Huckleberry Pancakes

The thrill of finding a *real* ghost town, not a restored one, is beyond description. After discovering one such remnant in Canada we were fascinated with the old buildings and corrals. To find a flourishing huckleberry patch was "icing on the cake."

Prepare two cups of your favorite pancake mix. Add one teaspoon sugar. Wash one cup huckleberries and drain them well. Fold gently into the pancake batter. Cook as you would for regular pancakes, using extra precaution in turning, so as not to mash the puffed up huckleberries. Serve with regular syrup or fruit syrup.

Maple Syrup
(makes 1 cup)

½ cup water
1 cup sugar
1 teaspoon Mapeline flavoring

Bring water to a boil. Add sugar and flavoring and stir until dissolved. Store in a jar. Warm to serve.

Also serve with fruit syrups (recipe on page 60) made with fresh fruit you may find along the way.

Custard Sauce for Fresh Berries
(makes approximately 3 cups sauce)

Serve berries in bowls with custard sauce for dessert.

1 package (3¾ oz.) instant vanilla pudding	2 cups milk
	1½ teaspoons vanilla
	1 cup heavy cream

Combine ingredients and beat with a rotary beater until smooth and slightly thickened. Serve over berries.

Any extra custard may be stored in the refrigerator. It will thicken. The next time you serve the custard, spoon in bowls and put the berries on top of the custard. Custard will keep three to four days.

Steamed Clams

If you are lucky enough to dig your own clams, steam them and serve with the broth. If you are not "digging," buy them and enjoy in a beach atmosphere.

We would suggest eight to twelve clams per person depending on individual appetites. The following recipe will serve four people.

clams	½ teaspoon garlic salt
3 cups water—or enough to just barely cover	1 tablespoon parsley
	1 lemon—cut in wedges
⅓ cup butter	melted butter

Clean and scrub clams in cold water. Be sure all sand is removed. Put clams in a deep pan. Add water, butter, garlic salt and parsley. Cover and steam until clams open. Remove clams and serve broth in a separate cup. Have melted butter for dipping and a lemon wedge for flavor. Rub your hands with the left over lemon to remove the clam odor.

Wild Asparagus

One of my fondest memories is going wild asparagus hunting with my father. When traveling with our children it was such a revelation to me to watch them adapt to the art of finding these delicacies with such ease.

The time of year to look for wild asparagus is the latter part of April, the month of May and the early part of June. The states in which we have found it arc Wisconsin, Minnesota, Michigan, northern Illinois and parts of Iowa. You may find it in other states as well, but these will give you a head start. The places to look are along fences by the side of the roads. It also grows around groups of trees. We have found it along both sides of the road but the old-timers *who know* say, "It's in confined areas, ya' know, and it sometimes grows in patches." "Depends on the wind, ya' know, but for the best 'uns look on the south side of the fence on a road runnin' east and west. Look on the east side of the road runnin' north and south."

Look for some stalks. If they have gone to flower or "laced out" they are tough and not good eating. If you find a tall stalk with several shoots off to the sides, break off the tips three to five inches from the end.

Once you are in the right area and you have spotted an asparagus stalk, walk along the fence, careful that you don't step on a sprout. Look for the white tip pushing up through the leaves and grasses. When you find one, look further. You may find leaves and grasses. When you find one, look further. You may find only one or you could find as many as ten to twelve. Brush away the leaves and grass. Take a sharp knife and cut at an angle about one inch down into the soil. If the tip is three to five inches high you've got the best thing you've ever tasted. Continue walking, hunting and cutting until you have ten to twelve per person.

Lay the asparagus in the bottom of a sauce pan. Cover with boiling salted water and simmer fifteen to twenty minutes until just tender. Serve with melted butter.

Looking for the wild-growing abundance of nature as you travel can really be a rewarding experience for kids and grown-ups alike. Once you've developed a keen sense for where to look and what to look for, it becomes second nature.

We now understand why our offspring seemed to grasp the basics of botany and biology so easily in school later.

41

BREAKFAST CAN BE——

The day's beautiful beginning. Whether eaten in the early dawn or long after the sun has risen, our first meal of the day nourishes our bodies and our spirits. It sort of sets the pace for the day.

Some of the most memorable places we have eaten breakfast come to mind. When we visit our youngest daughter, who is in college at San Luis Obispo, we have a stretch of beach miles long to choose from. One morning we drove high up in the hills overlooking the Pacific. We found a huge craggy rock with a hollow center. We set up our chairs in the center and were protected against the wind. As we prepared our eggs and juice, we took turns with the binoculars to watch a group of seals at play. Truly, the world was our oyster.

One night we were very late getting away for our weekend away from it all. We drove to Ojai, California, to a campground we had remembered seeing several years ago. It was pitch-dark when we arrived. The campground roads were very winding and seemed to go up and down. We finally reached the crest of a high hill and decided to stop. We were in a perfect spot, just under a magnificent pine tree and could see thousands of twinkling lights in the distance below. We had been working rather steadily during the week so we were very lazy the next morning. Completely relaxed without a care in the world, we laid in bed while the coffee brewed. Sipping steaming mugs of coffee and enjoying our quiet time, we pulled back the curtains to survey our surroundings. It was breathtaking. We commented that it must be "Shangri-la."

Later in the day as we wandered through the quaint shops in town, we told one of the shopkeepers how much we had enjoyed our stay and that we had felt like we had been in paradise when we saw the beautiful view from our campsite. "Oh you were!" she said. She went on to explain that the Shangri-la in the movie *Lost Horizon* was filmed from the spot we had parked our motor home the night before.

While staying by the side of a lake in the interior of British Columbia we decided to row out to a tiny island for a breakfast picnic. We packed our feast and set out just as the sun was peeping over the trees. The water was like glass and the deepest blue-green imaginable. Loons were diving near our little boat. Magnificent! The lush green growth made it a bit difficult to negotiate a landing but we finally made it. We fell in love with the island. When we returned we asked a fisherman, "Who owns the island?" "Oh, no one can own that island, it's the Queen's property." Lovely, to eat a breakfast fit for a king on the Queen's island.

Even if you don't have your breakfast on an isolated island belonging to the Queen of England, or nestled above a beautiful valley good enough to call Shangri-la, breakfast in the outdoors in a camper can equal those enjoyed anywhere. Your frame of mind has a lot to do with it.

Things to Choose From

JUICES—
  fresh-squeezed orange juice
  grapefruit juice
  tomato juice
  apple juice
  pineapple juice

MEAT—
  bacon
  ham
  sausage
  steak
  pork chops
  Canadian bacon

FRUITS—
  orange halves
  grapefruit halves
  orange and grapefruit sections mixed together
  fresh pineapple wedges
  melon or a blend of several melons
  cooked fruits—prunes, apricots etc.
  fresh sliced peaches and cream
  whole strawberries
  raspberries
  blueberries

EGGS—
  roasted
  boiled
  poached
  scrambled
  fried
  baked
  omelets

CEREALS—
  cold cereal
  hot cereal

BREAD—
  toast
  muffins
  biscuits
  pancakes
  English muffins
  French toast
  coffee cake
  sweet rolls

SIDE ORDERS—
  hash brown potatoes
  grits
  corn beef hash
  country gravy
  fish
  jams and jellies
  fruit syrups

Cold Cereal

Take several of the variety packs. Some can be eaten right out of the box. Saves on cleanup. Make up a blend of several favorites at home and package for travel.

1 box Rice Chex
1 box Wheat Chex
1 box Ralstons

Blend together and eat as one cereal.

1 box Corn Flakes
1 box Grape Nut Flakes
1 box Wheaties

Blend together and eat as one cereal.

Granola

A good project to start thinking about "getting ready." Some cool morning out on the trail you'll be glad you did. After a hike before breakfast to Angel Falls, we were all out of energy and a big bowl of granola tasted mighty good.

3 tablespoons cooking oil	¾ cup dry roasted peanuts
3 cups rolled oats—regular not instant	1 cup seedless raisins
¼ cup toasted sesame seeds	¼ cup dates
¼ cup wheat germ	¼ cup figs—not fresh
½ cup pretoasted coconut	¼ cup dried apricots
	¼ cup dried peaches

Mix oil into oats and spread evenly on a baking sheet. Bake in a 250° oven until golden brown, checking after fifteen minutes and every two minutes thereafter. Watch closely so that it does not burn. Cool. Add sesame seeds, wheat germ and coconut. Chop peanuts very fine and add. Add raisins and toss to blend well. Chop dates, figs, apricots and peaches into small pieces and blend in thoroughly. Store in airtight containers until ready to use.

Five or Seven Grain Cereal

These can be purchased at most health food stores. Either is delicious and nutritious, a welcome change from oatmeal and cream of wheat. It does take a little longer to cook but it is well worth it. We particularly like the nutty flavor of the seven grain.

Muffin Tin Breakfast

Don't forget, many egg dishes can also be served for lunch or dinner. Serve one or two per person.

    1 strip bacon for each section of the tin
    1 egg for each section of the tin
    ½ teaspoon butter for each egg
    2 teaspoons cream for each egg
    salt and pepper to taste

45

Cook the bacon about two-thirds done. Drain. Cut off a piece about one inch in length from each strip. Lay these in the very bottom of each section of the muffin tin. Take the remaining long strips and lay them around the sides of the sections, overlapping the ends. Break an egg in the center of each section. Dot tops with butter. Pour the cream on each one and salt and pepper to taste. Bake in a 350° oven fifteen to twenty-five minutes, depending on how well done you like your eggs. They will lift out perfectly if you run a knife around the edges to loosen them.

If you do not have a muffin tin, shape foil into sections and put them in a cake pan. Grease the foil surfaces with the bacon drippings. They can be eaten right out of the foil cups.

Baked Eggs with Ham and Cheese

These can be baked in individual serving dishes or in one very large baking pan. A meal in itself. The ingredients are given for one person. Just multiply by the number of people to increase the recipe.

a buttered baking dish	2 eggs
1 teaspoon butter	1 tablespoon cream
1 thin slice ham	⅛ teaspoon paprika
1 thin slice Swiss cheese	salt and pepper to taste

Put butter in the dish. Layer the ham and cheese on top of each other. Break the eggs on the cheese. Add cream. Sprinkle paprika, salt and pepper on top. Bake in a 350° oven twelve to twenty minutes depending on how well done you desire the eggs.

Egg Cakes
(serves 3 or 4)

2 tablespoons butter	4 eggs
1 cup milk	2 cups broken saltine crackers
	¼ teaspoon seasoned pepper

Melt butter in a skillet. Add the milk. When milk is hot, break in the eggs and stir quickly with a fork. When the eggs begin to thicken add the crackers. Stir slightly and then cook until done without stirring. Season with seasoned pepper. Cut in wedges to serve.

Hearty Brunch

For that leisure time when everyone is sleeping in, you may want to have brunch (breakfast and lunch all in one) and later dinner. Served with fresh fruit this is a well-balanced meal. This dish will serve from four to six people.

6 slices bacon	6 eggs
1 medium onion	6 English muffin halves—
1 can tomatoes or 2 fresh ones	buttered and toasted

Fry bacon. Remove from skillet and drain. Save two tablespoons bacon drippings. Chop the onion and saute until transparent but not brown. Add tomatoes, if fresh cut into small pieces. Stir and cook about five minutes. Break the eggs into the simmering mixture and cook until set. Salt and pepper to taste. Lift out an egg and place on a toasted English muffin half. Spoon the rest of the mixture evenly over the tops.

Roasted Eggs

Simply put eggs in a 325° oven for twenty-five minutes. If you have a campfire, and we often do for the aesthetic value alone, lay the eggs you wish to roast near the fire. Turn every five minutes.

Eggs Benedict
(on the run)

1 small can hollandaise sauce	eggs
thin slices Canadian	English muffin
bacon—canned	halves—toasted

47

Heat the hollandaise in the opened can in a pan of hot water. Fry the bacon quickly in the bottom of a saucepan. Place bacon slices on toasted muffin halves, fill the same pan with water two-thirds full. Add a pinch of salt and a teaspoon of vinegar if you have it. Put the eggs, still whole in the shells, in the water when it begins to simmer. Leave them for about forty-five seconds. Remove them, swirl the water in a circle and break the eggs in the well in the middle. Cook the eggs one at a time. Lift out and lay on top of Canadian bacon and toasted English muffin. Pour hollandaise sauce over the top. Really quite a remarkable thing to enjoy in the comfort of your home-on-wheels.

Creamed Eggs on Toast
(serves 2)

1 small can white sauce	salt and pepper to taste
3 hard cooked eggs	4 slices wheat bread
¼ teaspoon parsley	butter

Heat white sauce and add eggs chopped coarse. Add parsley and salt and pepper. Butter the wheat bread and toast or grill. Lay one slice toast on each plate. Put a fourth the creamy mixture on each slice. Top with the second slice and pour the rest of the creamed mixture on top.

Paper Cup Omelets

The fillings will depend on what you happen to have on hand. The ones listed are suggestions only. Eggs, paper cups and canned milk are a necessity.

2 eggs per person	1 tablespoon canned milk per person
2 paper cups per person	a choice of fillings and they will vary from time to time

Fillings should be a choice of at least two or more from the following:

crumbled bacon	left over chopped ham
chopped mushrooms	sliced avocado
chopped green pepper	chopped chives
chopped green onions	cooked, boned fish broken in
chopped brown onions	small pieces
small cherry tomatoes—cut	any cooked vegetables
in half	cheese cut in cubes—several
crumbled corn beef	kinds

One of our favorite combinations is bacon, green pepper and cheddar cheese.

Put two eggs in a paper cup and add a tablespoon canned milk. Put the fillings of each individual's choice in another paper cup. It is fun to cook the omelets one at a time.

Each person can cook his own if they wish. Beat the eggs and milk with a fork. Pour in a very hot skillet which has been heated with one teaspoon butter melted in the center and rolled around. Lift the edges so that excess liquid can run underneath. Sprinkle the cup of filling into the center. Fold in half and roll out on your plate. It is a fun event and you may find you draw spectators.

Omelets make a great dinner. Try fresh asparagus or browned ground beef as a dinner filling.

Deluxe Scrambled Eggs

Here are a few things to add to scrambled eggs to make them an extra special treat.

1 to 2 eggs per person
1 teaspoon water to 2 eggs

Blend well and scramble in a hot skillet which has one tablespoon bacon drippings, butter or oil in it. Always add other ingredients to the slightly beaten eggs before putting in the skillet.

a few chopped mushrooms	**crumbled bacon**
canned bacon bits	**cream cheese—**
	cut into small pieces

Cranberry Fold

2 eggs per person
¼ cup whole berry cranberry sauce

Beat eggs until fluffy. Have a skillet with butter very very hot. Pour in eggs and shake pan several times. As soon as eggs solidify, add cranberry sauce in a row down the center. Fold over in half and turn out on a plate.

Eggs in a Basket

Made in a muffin tin, these eggs are easy and decorative too. There is a new product on the market called egg baskets. The package contains pieces of dough designed to fit in a muffin tin. For years our family has used a plain piece of bread. Try them both ways and take your choice.

1 piece of bread—crusts re-	**1 teaspoon butter**
moved or 1 section of egg	**1 egg**
basket dough	**salt and pepper to taste**

Butter the bread and push down into a section of the muffin tin. It will form a deep cup. Put the egg in the center and season with salt and pepper. Bake in a 350° oven twelve to fifteen minutes.

One-Eyed Egg

1 piece of bread
1 teaspoon butter
1 egg

Tear a hole from the center of the bread slice as round as possible Put butter in a skillet. As soon as the butter is melted put the bread with the hole in the center in the skillet. Break the egg in the hole. Cook until bread is browned and turn over to cook other side. Brown the round piece from the center and put over the hole to serve.

Fried Eggs with—

Fry an egg sunny side up or over easy. Serve plain or:

on toast	on a pork chop
on fried corn beef	with steak
on a slice of ham	on a tortilla
with cheese on top	with hash brown potatoes

Fried Breakfast

Prepare the filling at home. This recipe will make four fried breakfasts; double for eight.

4 slices bacon—cooked crisp and crumbled	1 teaspoon dry mustard
	½ cup mayonnaise
4 hard cooked eggs—grated	salt and pepper to taste.
¼ green pepper—chopped fine	¼ cup butter
2 tablespoons minced onion	8 slices bread.

Mix bacon, eggs, green pepper, onion, mustard, mayonnaise, salt and pepper together and store in covered container. At destination, butter one side of each slice of bread. Spread the filling on the unbuttered side and put together like a sandwich with the outsides buttered. Fry on both sides.

Fried Eggs in Corned Beef

Brown corned beef. Make depressions in the center. Break the eggs in the depression and cook till set. A good way to do this is to cover the pan. Serve on buttered toast. Season with salt and pepper and serve catsup on the side.

Eggs Rancheros
(serves 4 to 6)

1 can enchilada sauce
1 small can chopped green chili
  peppers

6 eggs
6 corn tortillas
¼ lb. jack cheese—grated or
  cubed

In a large skillet heat the enchilada sauce and green chilies. When it begins to bubble, break the eggs into the sauce one at a time. Cover and cook over low heat until eggs are set. Serve on a toasted corn tortilla with sauce over the top of the egg. Sprinkle with cheese.

Country Skillet Breakfast
(serves 4)

We began enjoying this while tent camping. It is such a favorite that we include it in all modes of travel on wheels.

½ lb. bacon—or more
2 large potatoes—baked and
  cooled

8 eggs
salt and pepper to taste

Fry bacon until crisp. Remove from pan. Save two tablespoons bacon drippings in the skillet. Cut the potatoes into small cubes and cover the bottom of the skillet. Let them brown, turning as needed. Beat the eggs together and pour over the potatoes. Crumble the bacon over the eggs. Stir, gently moving the mixture around to cook similar to scrambled eggs. Season with salt and pepper. Great with biscuits and honey.

French Toast

Any bread makes good French toast, but the real thing calls for one inch thick egg bread. We find it in markets all over the country. You can buy unsliced bread and slice it an inch thick also. Any bread not used as French toast is a perfect base for creamed chicken or fish. Also good buttered and grilled. Recipe below will make one thick slice of French toast or two thin ones.

1 egg	**¼ teaspoon sugar**
1 teaspoon cream	**1 teaspoon confectioner's sugar**

Beat egg, cream and sugar together. Pour in a flat dish. Lay the bread in and soak one-half minute, turn and soak one-half minute. All the egg mixture should soak into the bread. Fry in at least one-half inch oil in hot skillet. Remove and sprinkle confectioner's sugar on one side. Serve with syrup or jam.

Cinnamon Toss

Fry or grill bread on both sides in butter. Put the following into a brown paper bag:

½ cup confectioner's sugar
½ cup sugar
1 tablespoon cinnamon

Shake the bag to mix ingredients well. Put hot toast inside and shake to coat evenly.

Any biscuit or muffin recipe adds to the breakfast pleasure. If you have biscuits or muffins for dinner, make extra ones to split and toast for breakfast. Planned leftovers are a boon to time-saving cooking.

Maple Toast

1 slice bread	**2 teaspoons maple syrup**
1 teaspoon butter	**¼ teaspoon cinnamon**

Use half the butter to spread on one side of bread. Broil until nicely browned. Mix the rest of the butter, maple syrup and cinnamon together and spread on the untoasted side. Run back under the broiler to let the mixture heat and soak in.

Oatmeal Pancakes
(serves 4 to 6)

2 cups milk
2 cups minute oatmeal
2 eggs

2 teaspoons baking powder
¼ cup shortening
1 teaspoon salt
1 teaspoon sugar

Heat milk but do not let it boil. Stir in oatmeal until well blended and continue stirring one minute. Remove from fire and cool. Beat in rest of ingredients. Cook on a greased griddle, turning once. Serve with butter and syrup or butter and brown sugar.

Rice Griddlecakes

Another way to plan breakfast the night before. Just make sure to prepare an extra cup of rice.

1 cup flour
¾ teaspoon baking soda
1 cup cooked rice

1 egg—slightly beaten
1½ cups sour cream
2 tablespoons melted butter
1 teaspoon salt

Sift flour and soda together. Add rice, egg, sour cream, melted butter and salt. Stir until well-blended. Drop by spoonfuls onto a hot griddle. Turn once, browning on both sides. Serve with maple syrup or honey.

Cinnamon Biscuits

1 package refrigerator biscuits
¼ cup melted butter

2 teaspoons cinnamon
2 tablespoons sugar

Dip each biscuit into melted butter on both sides. Dip one side only in cinnamon and sugar that has been mixed together. Lay sugar side up in a round pie pan. The sides should be touching. Bake eight to ten minutes according to package directions.

Orange Coconut Buns

2 tablespoons sugar	2 tablespoons butter
2 tablespoons concentrated orange juice	½ cup flaked coconut
	1 package refrigerator biscuits

Mix sugar, orange juice (make the rest of the juice for drinking), butter together. Heat until sugar is dissolved. Add coconut and spread over biscuits in a pan. Bake according to package directions.

Variation: Use chopped nuts in place of the coconut.

Jam Crepes
(serves 4)

Use a packaged pancake mix or your own dry mix from home. Make the recipe for pancakes. Now comes the fun. After completing regular pancake recipe add:

2 eggs—slightly beaten
¼ cup additional milk

Whip until well blended. Heat a seven inch skillet. Brush with oil and pour in two to three tablespoons of the batter. It will be very thin. As it begins to cook, roll the skillet around letting the liquid run out to the edges. Turn once and immediately remove to a baking sheet. When all have been cooked, put jam in the center and roll up like a jelly roll. Lay folded edge down on a baking sheet. Heat for five minutes in a 350° oven.

After warming, sprinkle generously with confectioner's sugar. Sausage goes well with the crepes.

Quickest Coffee Cake Ever
(makes 1 eight inch pan)

⅓ cup sugar	1½ cups flour
¼ cup butter	2 teaspoons baking powder
1 egg	¼ teaspoon salt
⅔ cup milk	½ teaspoon vanilla

Beat sugar and butter until light and creamy. Add egg and milk and blend well. Sift flour, baking powder and salt together and add to creamed mixture. Add vanilla and blend. Pour into a buttered eight inch cake pan. Bake in a 350° oven twenty-five to thirty minutes.

Variation: Top the uncooked batter with butter, cinnamon, sugar and a few chopped nuts.

Apple Pancake
(serves 3 to 4)

¾ cup flour
3 tablespoons sugar
¼ teaspoon salt
3 eggs

¾ cup light cream
4 tablespoons butter—melted
3 large apples
2 tablespoons brown sugar
½ teaspoon cinnamon

Mix the flour, sugar, salt, eggs, cream and two tablespoons of the melted butter together in a bowl. Heat a ten inch cast iron skillet and brush with oil to prevent sticking. Pour in the batter and cook until set. Slice the apples and lay over the top completely covering the surface. Sprinkle with brown sugar and cinnamon that has been mixed together. Pour the remaining two tablespoons butter over all. Bake in a 400° oven six to eight minutes. Serve warm.

Hash Brown Potatoes

Plan extra baked potatoes for the evening meal. Save several for breakfast. Peel and grate the potatoes. Salt and pepper them generously. Heat one-fourth inch bacon drippings in a cast iron skillet. Add the potatoes and cook without stirring until bottom is browned. Add a half teaspoon paprika and toss around in the skillet until browned evenly.

Mashed Potato Pancakes

2 cups mashed potatoes—cold	**2 tablespoons flour**
2 eggs	**2 tablespoons melted butter**
	salt and pepper to taste.

Blend all together and cook like pancakes. Let one side brown thoroughly before turning.

Baked Cheese Grits
(serves 4 to 8)

The grits are cut in squares to serve so you can plan to cut smaller squares when you need to serve extra people. This may be prepared the night before and baked in the morning. One morning in a very cold thunderstorm the warmth from the oven was most welcome. The cheesy aroma made us feel snug as a bug in a rug.

1 cup grits	**1 cup diced sharp cheddar**
4 cups water	**cheese**
1 teaspoon salt	**2 eggs**
½ cup butter	**¼ cup corn flake crumbs—**
½ cup milk	**optional**

Cook grits in water with salt until done. Reduce heat and stir in butter and cheese until both are melted. Remove from fire. Beat milk and eggs together and stir into the grit mixture. Pour into a buttered baking pan and sprinkle with crumbs. Bake in a 325° oven thirty-five to forty minutes.

Red-Eye Gravy

True red-eye gravy needs country ham but you can make a milder version using any fried ham. Smoked ham is even better. To make the gravy, first fry the ham. Remove ham to a platter and turn up the fire. The skillet should be very hot. Add approximately one to one and a half cups boiling water to the skillet. It will sizzle and sputter but will eventually calm down. Scrape up all the bits of browned ham from the bottom and stir until the juices are reduced by about one-third. This whole process does not take very long. Serve in a bowl and let each person pour some over the ham.

Red-eye gravy over hot biscuits is finger-lickin' good.

Bacon Country Gravy

When the bacon is cooked, save the flavorful grease that remains. It is useful in many ways. Serve this excellent gravy on potatoes, macaroni, bread, biscuits and toast. For every cup of gravy you will need two tablespoons drippings.

2 tablespoons drippings	1 cup water
2 tablespoons flour	¼ teaspoon pepper

Heat the drippings and stir in the flour until you have a smooth paste. Brown the flour. Add the water and stir until it thickens. Season with pepper. The bacon is salty so taste before adding salt.

Milk Gravy

Our grandmothers, who happened to be third cousins, served this gravy every morning we can remember. The farmhands "ate it up" and so did we. I remember a platter of bacon and sausage stacked higher than I could see and a plate of biscuits twice as high. The bowl of milk gravy was always in the center of the table. The following recipe will yield two cups (a distinct compromise, of course).

¼ cup bacon drippings
¼ cup flour
2 cups milk

Heat the drippings and stir in the flour until you have a smooth paste. Do not brown. Add the milk at once and stir until smooth. Season as needed.

Variation: When serving for an evening meal, add two tablespoons dehydrated onion to the drippings before adding the flour.

Honey

Look for signs along the road. We have purchased many different varieties while traveling. Eucalyptus, all natural honey, is one of our favorites. We enjoy the thick kind with lots of honey comb. Sorghum is lovely. The children always say sorghum is like molasses. I agree with them only it is just "more so."

Jams and Jellies

The secret is fresh, really fresh fruit. Use only a small amount at a time. Two peaches will make enough for several days. After that you may want to try a new flavor. For jelly, mash the fruit to a pulp and beat with a fork to get it as smooth as possible. Measure the amount of fruit pulp and add one-third the amount of water. Add sugar until the fruit is sweet enough. Cook until thickened over medium heat. Store in the refrigerator. It will thicken even more. This is really a fruit butter rather than a clear jelly but the taste is full and fresh.

For jam, cut the fruit into fairly large pieces. Add water to barely cover the fruit in a sauce pan. Add sugar until the fruit and water are thickened and cloudy. One cup of fruit and one-fourth cup of sugar is a good proportion. Cook, stirring constantly, until the mixture boils down and becomes thickened. Cool.

Fresh Cranberry Sauce

Make to fill the Cranberry Fold or use as a jam for toast. Also great with chicken.

2 cups fresh cranberries
1 cup sugar
½ cup water

Cook until berries pop and mixture thickens. This takes about ten minutes. I remember one Thanksgiving my youngest daughter-in-law asked me why she never knew making your own cranberry sauce could be so easy. I told her, "somebody has to tell you." Somebody told me, somebody told her, Now, somebody told you.

Fruit Syrup

Fruit syrups are best made from ripe berries. The flavor of fruit syrups is one of the truest in the world.

2 cups fruit
1 cup sugar

Chop or mash the fruit. Add one cup sugar and stir until blended. Place in a warm place for two hours. An oven that was turned off an hour or so before is a good place. Don't forget and drive because it will slosh. Strain and save the fruit for jelly or in pies. To make a thickened syrup cook until slightly thickened.

Serve the plain uncooked syrup to flavor juices or pour over crushed ice.

Serve the thickened syrup over pancakes, toast or biscuits.

LUNCHES

Although that noon meal, commonly referred to as "lunch" seems to be as traditional as apple pie, there are times when this meal is as superfluous and undesirable as a mother-in-law on a honeymoon.

When traveling in our camper, lunch is subject to neglect for a variety of reasons. First, we usually feature breakfast, since that is the basis for the beginning of our day. Second, we are often so occupied with a strenuous activity schedule that it is forgotten. Third, we aren't that anxious to stay that busy with food preparation, preferring to busy ourselves with other things. In addition, since we all seem to be so active, our day ends earlier than when we are at home and consequently we plan an earlier dinner hour. This attitude and scheduling puts "lunch" at a very low priority.

There are times when we do honor the tradition however. When we do, we select from recipes which we refer to as "nibblers" and "snacks." Light, nonfilling foods can provide the perfect "bridge" between breakfast and the evening meal. If fresh air and heavy food are coupled together in the middle of the day, most of us tend to become a bit drowsy . . . perhaps even lethargic. We consider that a waste of time and certainly not the planned result. If you insist on *lunch* . . . by all means have it . . . enjoy it. Just don't blame us for missing the geese teaching their little offspring how to catch insects . . . while you're asleep. Lunch can be compromised to the event of soups, sandwiches or picnic fare. We only suggest that it be as simple as is satisfying.

Some Sandwiches

Have sandwiches often. Have unusual sandwiches. Have sandwiches packed for an impromptu picnic. There are breakfast sandwiches, lunch sandwiches and dinner sandwiches. Even snack sandwiches and party sandwiches.

Use exotic breads, different spreads, new condiments and old stand-bys. Experiment!

We list some of our favorites. We hope to whet both your appetite and your creativity.

Where to serve sandwiches? Anywhere! Serve 'em in a bag, in a box and on a plate. Serve 'em by the lake, on a table and in bed. Plan a picnic for any meal. Eat 'em driving along in the rain or lounging in the sunshine.

Fishwiches

Sesame buns
4 fish sticks—per sandwich
mayonnaise

garlic salt
sweet relish
lettuce

Open the buns and lay on a flat surface. Grill the fish sticks until very hot. Mix mayonnaise, garlic salt and relish together and spread on both sides of the open buns. Lay the hot fish sticks close together on one bun. Top with lettuce. Close bun and serve while warm.

Beef Dip Sandwiches
(makes 10 to 12)

10 to 12 sour dough rolls—approx. 8" in length
1 three to four pound beef brisket
1 package Au-jus seasoning mix

The buns should be of a fairly soft variety. Cook the brisket in a 250° oven for six hours covered. Test with a fork. The meat should be very tender. Slice cross grain. The meat will come apart and be somewhat stringy. Open the buns and pile the meat on one-half evenly divided between the buns. Dip one half in the juice in the pan. Put the buns together and wrap in foil. Add the Au-jus mix to the juices left in the skillet the brisket was cooked in. Add water according to package directions. Scrape the browned bits from the bottom of the pan and simmer slowly for five minutes. Heat the wrapped sandwiches and the beef au-jus. Serve the au-jus in a bowl. Dip the sandwiches in the juice as you eat them. Obviously they are delicious eaten immediately or they will keep well several days in the refrigerator or weeks in the freezer.

Salad Sandwiches

Serve open face and use any bread of your choice, toasted.

cottage cheese	alfalfa sprouts
chopped chives	shredded lettuce
grated onion	garlic salt
grated carrot	paprika
	blue cheese dressing

Layer in order given in amounts of your choice.

Miniature BLT's

bread	cherry tomatoes
mayonnaise	canned bacon bits
lettuce	lemon pepper
	salt to taste

Cut a slice of bread in fourths, making four even squares. Spread with mayonnaise. Cut a piece of lettuce to fit on the bread. Cut a cherry tomato in half and lay on lettuce. Sprinkle bacon bits on top. Add pepper and salt to taste. Some may not need salt because the bacon will vary in saltiness. Make a platterful.

Black and White Club

2 slices white bread	sliced chicken
1 slice dark bread	swiss cheese
mayonnaise	sliced ham
mustard	sliced American cheese
	lettuce

Spread mayonnaise on one side of both slices of white bread. Spread mustard on both sides of dark bread. On one slice of white bread layer chicken, swiss cheese and lettuce. Top with dark bread. Layer ham, American cheese and lettuce on dark bread. Top with slice of white. Cut diagonally in half and diagonally in half again, making four triangles. If you want to be extra fancy, secure each quarter with a toothpick with an olive on top.

Variations: Try creations using bacon, tomato and butter.

Breakfast Sandwiches
(serves 4)

Eight sandwiches allows two per person.

8 slices toast	8 eggs—fried hard
butter for toast	8 slices cheese
	8 slices bacon

Lay toast on a baking sheet in single layer. Lay fried eggs and cheese on top. Fry bacon half done. Cut each piece in half and lay crisscross on top of cheese. Run under broiler until bacon is crisp and cheese is melted.

Diet Sandwich Rolls

butter lettuce	bologna—or any luncheon
cottage cheese	meat
dill	dill pickle
	mustard

64

Open the outer leaves of the lettuce and press flat with the palm of your hand. Spread with a thin layer of cottage cheese and season with the dill. Lay the bologna on top and as much dill pickle as you wish. Carefully roll edges together and secure with a toothpick.

French Fried Tuna
(makes 4 to 6 sandwiches)

8 to 12 slices bread
1 small onion
¼ cup chopped celery
8 ounces flaked and drained
  tuna fish

¼ cup mayonnaise
salt and pepper to taste
3 eggs
¾ cup milk
4 to 6 teaspoons butter
1 can condensed cheese soup

Lay bread out in a single layer. Chop the onion very fine and mix with the celery, tuna, mayonnaise, salt and pepper. Spread on half of the bread slices and top with the other half. Press together. Mix the eggs and milk together. Dip both sides of the sandwiches in this mixture and fry in butter until golden. Heat the soup and ladle some over the top of each fried sandwich.

Spread Burgers
(serves 4 to 6)

Use leftover chicken, turkey, beef or canned meat. Served with a salad and dessert, the meal is complete.

1 can condensed mushroom
  soup
1 cup diced cooked chicken
¼ cup sliced water chestnuts

¼ cup thinly sliced celery
¼ cup chopped green onions
1 teaspoon soy sauce
4 to 6 toasted English
  muffins—or buns

Mix first six ingredients together and blend well. Spread mixture over the bun to edges. Broil about four inches from heat about seven minutes. Serve with cranberry sauce.

Cheese Dreams

1 lb. cheddar cheese—grated
½ cup light cream
1 tablespoon Worcestershire
 saucé
½ teaspoon hot sauce—
 optional

¼ teaspoon garlic salt
salt and pepper to taste
½ teaspoon chopped
 parsley—optional
2 egg whites—beaten stiff

Blend all ingredients together until you have a smooth paste. Store in the refrigerator until ready to use. Spread liberally between bread slices and grill on both sides in melted butter.

Peanut Butter and:

grated raw carrot and lemon
 juice
chopped salted peanuts
raisins
chopped walnuts
two kinds of jelly
sliced red onion
dill pickles
cream cheese
ham

honey
crisp bacon
mayonnaise
lettuce
cheddar cheese
swiss cheese
apple butter
cucumber slices
olives
chili sauce

On: crackers, breads, toast, fruits, biscuits and all by itself.

Make Your Own at Home

1 cup peanuts
2 tablespoons vegetable oil
¼ teaspoon salt

Put in an electric blender and mix until smooth. Store in covered container. If it separates, just stir before using.

THE EVENING MEAL

This is usually our hearty one for the day. On some of our early cross-country treks we traveled by car. We discovered we enjoyed having our "evening meal around 4:00 p.m. The restaurants were not crowded and could usually seat the six of us. Then we drove on through the twilight, one of my favorite times of the day.

Indulge whenever your schedule suits you best. All the recipes in this section are "dinner" oriented. When touring the state of Alaska we found we were starving and wondered why? We had not realized how late in the evening darkness descended. We found ourselves eating our evening meal around 10:00 p.m. in bright sunlight.

If you prefer an omelet from the breakfast section, or a bowl of soup from the soup section or a sandwich while watching the sunset, switch your eating habits for your pleasure and enjoyment.

It is nice to prepare the evening meal before doing the breakfast dishes. You use the utensils to their best advantage and you'll have more time to enjoy the scenery when you stop for the night. I always feel as though I am going out for dinner when it is ready for the oven ahead of time.

Make it easy on yourself. Spend only as much time as you really want preparing the meal.

Stuffed Rock Cornish Hens

small rock cornish hens
1 package stuffing mix
oven roasting bags—or aluminum foil

Clean the hens and pat dry. Prepare the stuffing according to package directions. Stuff the cavity two-thirds full. Place in oven roasting bag or wrap in foil. Bake in a 300° oven for forty-five minutes to one hour.

When ready to serve, thicken the juices and serve as a gravy.

Variations: Brush with butter and seasoned salt and cook over an open fire, turning often.

Pigs in a Blanket
(makes 8 to 10)

Make extra ones and store in foil. Reheat the next day for lunch.

1 package refrigerator biscuits	**1 can Vienna sausages**
or	**butter**
1 recipe biscuits from a mix	**mustard**

Roll individual biscuits flat. Lay one sausage inside and roll up, completely enclosing the sausage. Lay seam side down on a baking surface. Bake in a 375° oven twelve to fifteen minutes. Serve with butter and mustard.

Cheese Rarebit
(serves 4)

Our daughter adores her rarebit served over crackers. Our youngest son prefers toast. We like toasted English muffins. We draw straws to see how it is to be served.

2 cans cheese soup
½ pound yellow cheese
½ teaspoon onion salt

¼ teaspoon paprika
½ can beer
8 slices bacon
crackers, toast, or muffins

Heat soup in a sauce pan without adding any water. Cut cheese in small pieces and add to soup. Stir until chunks are melted. Add onion salt, paprika and beer. Keep hot but do not boil. Cook bacon crisp and drain. Lay crackers on a plate. Put the bacon strips, two for each person, on top. Pour the rarebit over all.

Kidney Bean Stew
(serves 4)

1 lb. ground beef
1 small onion—chopped
1 strip bacon—cut in small
    pieces

1 can dark red kidney beans
1 can tomatoes
1 small can green peas
salt and pepper to taste

Brown beef in a skillet. Add chopped onion and bacon. Cook until all ingredients are nicely browned. Add kidney beans, tomatoes, green peas and salt and pepper. Cook until hot and serve in bowls.

Scotch Stew
(serves 4)

Serve Scotch stew over rice or potatoes. The mixture makes a marvelous filling on buns. It is unusual in its preparation and cooking time. It is sometimes difficult to wait for the finished product.

1 lb. ground beef
½ cup butter
½ cup catsup

Put all ingredients in a sauce pan. Stir until butter is melted and all ingredients are well blended. Do *not* brown the meat. Cover tightly and cook over the lowest heat for four hours. Stir occasionally to prevent sticking.

Stew from Cans

There are times when there is not a store within miles, which is one of the joys of travel. We have often planned to spend one day arriving at a certain spot on the map, but have found reasons to delay and dally along the way.

Driving along back logging roads in Alberta, B.C., we found a private campground. The year before we arrived, a flood had washed through the area changing the course of the river.

Bulldozers had been hard at work shaping new and better parking spaces and were finishing for the day. The owner asked us if we would be his first guests. We jumped at the invitation. The necessary ingredients are always packed with us for just such occasions. Whenever we have stew from cans, we replenish the larder at the next food stop.

4 slices bacon	1 small can tomatoes
1 can beef meat	1 can tomato soup
1 can small potatoes	¼ teaspoon garlic salt
1 can small onions	1 tablespoon chopped parsley
1 can mixed vegetables	salt and pepper to taste
	1 to 2 cups water as needed

Brown bacon in a large kettle. Break into small pieces. Add all the rest of the ingredients and simmer covered for one to two hours. Add water as needed. Sometimes the liquid from the canned ingredients is more abundant than usual and less water is required. Serve with French bread, sheepherder's bread or corn bread.

Hobo Dinners

Make these individual dinners after breakfast. If you have a freezer, make up several and freeze at home. Take them along for the evenings you want freedom. Recipe is for one.

¼ **pound ground beef**	**1 small carrot**
1 medium potato	**salt and pepper to taste**
½ **medium onion**	**1 tablespoon water**
	large square of aluminum foil

Shape the ground beef into a patty and brown (use the breakfast skillet). Lay the patty in the middle of the foil. Slice the potato and onion into thin slices and arrange over top. Cut the carrot into quarters lengthwise and cut strips to fit over the potato and onion. Salt and pepper to taste. Pour the tablespoon of water over the middle of the stack. Crimp the edges of the foil so the mixture is sealed. Store in the refrigerator until ready to use.

Remember that the meat patty is browned, not cooked completely, so it only takes a minute to make up these packets.

Bake in a 350° oven forty-five minutes if unfrozen, and an hour to an hour and fifteen minutes if frozen. Serve on paper plates and let each person eat from the packet. A great dinner to take outside the vehicle for an evening picnic.

Tex-Mex

This is a term given to Mexican food in the United States by many Mexican tourists. We seem to "re-do" the Mexican dishes to the accepted taste of the mass gringos. This is a little something I concocted and as it didn't have a name and the recipe did not come from Mexico, Tex-Mex it is.

I consider Tex-Mex a Mexican-like dish. It is quite good and you may vary the hot sauce to your own taste.

6 small flour tortillas
2 left-over fried chicken thighs
or drumsticks
¾ cup chopped onion
2 tablespoons butter
6 tablespoons taco sauce
2 tablespoons water

1 pound jack cheese
1 can green chili salsa (7 to 8
oz.)
¼ teaspoon oregano—fresh or
dried
½ teaspoon garlic seasoning
serve with warmed, buttered
flour tortillas if desired

Lay the six flour tortillas out on a flat surface. Chop the chicken into small pieces and mix with the chopped onion. Brown in the butter. Divide evenly in the middle of the tortillas. Put one tablespoon taco sauce on each tortilla. Grate the jack cheese and put two tablespoons on each tortilla. Save the rest. Roll the tortillas with the filling inside and place seam side down in a baking dish. A pottery one is "more Mexican." Add two tablespoons water. Pour on the green chili salsa. Sprinkle the oregano and garlic seasoning over all and top with the remaining jack cheese. Bake in a 300° oven for thirty to forty minutes until bubbly and lightly browned.

Serve with the buttered tortillas and add more hot sauce if desired. Hot sauce is any hot sauce of your choice. A mild taco sauce or a hot jalapeño chili sauce.

Samoan Pineapple Roast

1 #2 can sliced pineapple
1 small, canned ham
1 cup teriyaki marinade

aluminum foil or parchment
wrap
18 inch length household twine
1 length coat hanger wire
2 metal coat buttons

Drain juices from pineapple and reserve for fruit drinks later. Using the pineapple can as a "cutter," cut rounds of ham which have been sliced to the same thickness as pineapple slices. Alternate slices of ham and pineapple, ultimately having a ham slice on each end. Tie one button onto end of the twine. Use the length of coat hanger wire as a "needle" and run twine through the center of the "roast," tying off the opposite end and securing with the second button. Tie tightly.

Line a roasting pan with aluminum foil or parchment paper so that ends may be folded over to cover. Marinate the roast with teriyaki marinade for several hours, basting regularly. Preheat oven to 375° and bake for one hour. Fold back covering and bake for an additional ten to fifteen minutes.

Place on a serving platter garnished with mint leaves or parsley. Snip off the buttons and remove twine. The carving is already accomplished. Grind ham "trimmings" into ham-salad for later use for sandwiches.

This is a particularly good "do-ahead" main dish for an evening meal. If prepared at home, wrap in aluminum foil and store in the refrigerator of the camper for up to four or five days.

Pineapple Burgers
(serves four)

1 can pineapple slices—well-drained	salt and pepper to taste
1½ lbs. lean ground beef	½ cup bread crumbs
	2 eggs

Mix ground beef, eggs, seasonings and bread crumbs together. Form thin rounds of this mixture and place a slice of pineapple on top. Put another round of beef on top and pinch edges together well and form one large patty.

Fry in a hot skillet until well-browned. Serve on toasted, whole grain buns.

Variations: Substitute for the pineapple slice: cheddar cheese slice, jack cheese slice, thick slice tomato, thick slice onion.

Golden Baked Pork Chops
(for 4 to 6 pork chops)

4 to 6 pork chops
1 large onion—sliced thin

1 can golden mushroom soup
salt and pepper to taste

In a baking dish, layer in the order given. Bake in a 325° oven forty-five minutes. No need to cover. Serve with rice or potatoes.

Creole for Two

It's raining outside and the fog is rolling in. Our spirits are not damp. We have the table set and the candle lit. This trip out the kids are at home with a sitter.

2 tablespoons stuffed green
  olives
2 hard cooked eggs
1 small can stewed tomatoes
1 small can shrimp

1 package Spanish rice mix
¼ cup butter
¼ cup chopped onion
1 tablespoon chopped green
  pepper

Prepare rice according to package directions. Melt butter in a skillet. Add onion and green pepper and sauté for three minutes. Add olives, sliced in half, eggs, cut in pieces, tomatoes, and shrimp. Simmer ten minutes. Serve over rice.

Five Pound Pot Roast

A day of sightseeing can be exhausting. Nothing restores our strength more than the aroma of our dinner as we enter our home away from home.

Many people we have talked with who have electrical wiring are taking a crock pot along. If you do not have an oven or if you wish to use a crock pot, this recipe works well. We have also simmered it slowly on top of a burner with good results.

5 lb. pot roast
1 package onion soup mix

2 cans cream of celery soup
½ soup can sherry wine

Brown pot roast quickly on both sides. Sprinkle the soup mix on the top side. Spread the canned soup, undiluted, over the dry mix. Pour the sherry evenly over all. Cover tightly.Bake in a 250° oven six hours. Same for the crock pot. Top of the burner will take about an hour less cooking time.

Variation: Substitute mushroom soup, red wine, stew beef for pot roast and cut cooking time in half.

Fish au Gratin
(serves 4 to 8 depending on fish)

3 tablespoons butter
1 carrot—chopped
1 celery stalk—sliced
1 small onion—chopped
1 clove garlic—minced
1 teaspoon parsley—chopped
1 teaspoon chopped chives
¼ teaspoon basil
¼ teaspoon dill

¼ teaspoon paprika
salt and pepper to taste
2 or more cups cooked, cubed
  fish
2 cans condensed cream of
  potato soup
½ cup white wine— or water
1 tablespoon butter
1 tablespoon lemon juice
½ cup cracker crumbs

Don't let the list of ingredients fool you into thinking the recipe is difficult. It is easy and can be done ahead of time or on the road.

Melt three tablespoons butter and sauté the carrot, celery, onion and garlic until tender. Add parsley, chives, basil, dill, paprika, salt and pepper. Blend well. Pour in the bottom of baking dish. Lay the fish over this mixture. Pour soup mixed with wine over the fish. Dot with one tablespoon butter. Sprinkle with lemon juice and cracker crumbs. Cover and bake in a 350° oven twenty-five minutes. Uncover and bake ten minutes longer.

Grilled Trout

Trout caught in fresh mountain streams need nothing added to make them delicious. Tory Wretman, the famous restaurateur from Sweden, once asked a Laplander his secret preparation for salmon. "There is no secret," he replied, "why should I do anything to it, it is perfect like it is."

6 cleaned trout

Grill over an open fire.

Sierra Grill

Prepare the coating mix and store in plastic container. This recipe will be enough to coat twelve to fourteen trout.

1 cup yellow cornmeal	**¼ teaspoon monosodium**
⅓ cup flour	**glutamate—optional**
½ teaspoon salt	**⅛ teaspoon garlic salt**
⅛ teaspoon seasoned pepper	**1 teaspoon chopped parsley**
	½ teaspoon paprika

Sift cornmeal and flour together. Add the rest of the ingredients. And mix evenly in shallow pan. Dredge the trout through the mixture, coating both sides. Grill or fry. Do not overcook. The trout is done when the meat is white and the bones pull away from the backbone. If frying in a skillet use enough oil to sizzle up around the trout.

Chili Trout

Brush with butter and sprinkle chili powder over both sides of the trout. Grill or fry.

Baked Fish
(makes enough for 4 to 8)

Use any fish desired. Catch your own or buy from local fish markets or fishermen on fishing piers.

Lay fish in the bottom of a baking dish or in aluminum foil. Cover with the following sauce and bake in a 350° oven twenty to thirty minutes.

1 cup sour cream	**½ teaspoon salt**
¼ cup Parmesan cheese	**¼ teaspoon seasoned pepper**
1 tablespoon lemon juice	**¼ teaspoon paprika**
1 teaspoon grated onion	**½ teaspoon chopped parsley**

Mix together and pour over fish.

Variation: Use same recipe for chicken or veal.

Paprika Chicken

We usually prepare two chickens instead of one and use the second one as an elegant cold picnic the following day. You may substitute all legs, all thighs, all breasts or any combination for the whole chicken. Deboned breasts are a real luxury. Use the bones for soup. The following recipe is for one large cut-up chicken or its equivalent in single pieces.

1 chicken cut up—with or	**½ teaspoon paprika**
** without skin**	**¼ teaspoon garlic salt**
½ cup butter	**¼ teaspoon monosodium**
	** glutamate—optional**

Keep the chicken in the refrigerator or freezer until ready to use. Melt the butter and add seasonings. Stir to blend well. Dip each piece of chicken in the hot mixture and lay in foil on a baking sheet. The cold chicken will let the hot mixture coat each piece of chicken evenly. Bake in a 350° oven one hour.

Variation: Seal the foil and bake. The chicken will not be as crisp. It is more moist and the juices make excellent gravy when thickened.

Italian Chicken

2 lbs. frying chicken—cut in pieces
1 package Italian salad dressing
⅓ cup grapefruit juice
¼ teaspoon grated grapefruit peel—optional
⅓ cup salad oil

Lay chicken pieces in a pan. Mix the rest of the ingredients and pour over the chicken pieces. Marinate overnight or all day. Broil or cook over open fire, turning frequently. Baste with marinade while cooking.

Citrus Glazed Chicken

8 chicken breasts or 8 legs and thighs
1 tablespoon kitchen bouquet
¼ cup honey
¼ cup concentrated orange juice

Lay chicken pieces on aluminum foil on a baking sheet. Combine remaining ingredients and brush over chicken pieces. Bake in a 375° oven forty to fifty minutes. Brush with remaining glaze during baking.

Burgundy Stew
(serves 4)

1 lb. stew beef—cut into one inch chunks
½ cup burgundy—or any red wine
1 can condensed consommé (10½ oz. can)
¾ teaspoon salt
⅛ teaspoon pepper
1 onion—sliced
¼ cup fine dry bread crumbs
¼ cup flour

Combine beef, wine, consommé, salt, pepper and sliced onion in a casserole dish. Blend crumbs and flour and sprinkle over mixture. Stir in slightly. Cover and bake in a 300° oven two and a half to three hours or until tender. Serve with noodles.

Corned Beef Deluxe
(serves 6 to 8)

2 cups cooked potatoes—diced	3 hard-cooked eggs—sliced
salt and pepper to taste	2 cups white sauce—may be
½ teaspoon paprika	canned
1 can corned beef (12 oz. size)	1 cup grated cheese
1 large onion—sliced thin	3 tablespoons melted butter
	⅓ cup bread crumbs

Place potatoes in a greased casserole dish. Season with salt, pepper and paprika. Layer the corned beef, onions and eggs on top of the potatoes. Mix cream sauce and cheese together and pour over the layered mixture. Stir the melted butter and bread crumbs together and sprinkle over the top. Bake in a 350° oven thirty to thirty-five minutes.

Spicy Beef on a Bun
(serves 4)

Double the recipe and wrap the extra ones in foil. Freeze and reheat at a later date. If you do not have a freezer, the wrapped buns will keep several days.

1 lb. ground beef	1½ tablespoons vinegar
½ cup uncooked oatmeal	1 tablespoon sugar
1½ teaspoons salt	½ cup catsup
½ cup evaporated milk	¼ cup water
1 tablespoon Worcestershire sauce	3 medium onions—chopped

Mix the ground beef, oatmeal, salt and milk together. Shape into patties. Brown in a skillet, turning once. Mix the rest of the ingredients together and pour over the meat patties. Bake in a 325° oven forty minutes. If you don't have an oven, cook on a top burner, stirring and turning as necessary. Serve on buns.

Also serve open-face on toast.

Skilletini

When cooking for a crowd, consider Skilletini. Once during each summer, each of the children want to take a friend along. So we pack the extra sleeping bags and the Skilletini.

1 lb. link sausage
1 lb. ground beef
1 cup chopped celery
1 cup chopped onion
1 cup chopped green pepper
1 large can tomatoes
1 can mushrooms—sliced (7 to 8 oz. size)
½ teaspoon garlic salt
1 tablespoon Worcestershire sauce
1 tablespoon sugar
1 teaspoon salt
¼ teaspoon seasoned pepper
½ cup chopped parsley
½ lb. spaghetti
½ lb. cheddar cheese

Slice sausage and brown in a large cast iron skillet or dutch oven. Add ground beef and brown. Add celery, onion and green pepper. Cover and simmer eight minutes. Add tomatoes, mushrooms and seasonings. Cover and simmer ten minutes. Add parsley. Break spaghetti into pieces and push them under the sauce. Cover and simmer over lowest heat thirty to forty minutes. Check occasionally to prevent sticking. If mixture seems dry, add a little water. Grate the cheese and sprinkle over the top. Let melt down before serving. If you have an oven, run the skillet under the broiler to melt cheese.

French Meat Loaf

1 lb. ground beef
½ cup garlic French dressing
2 tablespoons flour
¼ teaspoon salt
¼ teaspoon paprika
⅛ teaspoon pepper
2 tablespoons butter

Mix the ground beef and garlic French dressing together. Cover and refrigerate overnight. Shape into a meat loaf or if you prefer, individual ones. Mix the flour, salt, paprika and pepper together and dust the entire meat loaf. Melt the butter and quickly sear the meat loaf on all sides. Bake in a 325° oven forty-five minutes to one hour.

Variation: Form into flat patties and grill over open fire or charcoal. Serve in buns.

Both versions are served with the following sauce.

French Sauce

½ cup finely chopped onion   ½ cup mayonnaise
½ teaspoon horseradish   ½ cup mustard

Blend all ingredients together until creamy. Serve on the meat loaf or patties in buns. We take along dry horseradish and reconstitute as needed.

Chili Burrito

After a hard day of filming and house cleaning, we had planned to dine out. The nearest restaurant had closed and it was twenty miles to the next town. At 10:30 p.m. we sat down and devoured this dish for the very first time. We never have Chili Burrito, on the road or at home, without remembering that evening.

1 can chili   ½ lb. ground beef
1 cup jack cheese—grated   1 medium onion—chopped
½ cup water   8 flour tortillas

Brown the ground beef. Evenly divide the browned meat and the chopped onions in the center of each tortilla. Roll them up and lay fold side down in a 9 inch x 13 inch baking pan. Pour the chili over the top. Sprinkle the grated cheese over the chili. Pour the water over all. Bake in a 350° oven thirty to forty minutes.

Cheese Strata
(makes a 9 inch x 13 inch pan)

Compare with a delicate cheese souffle. It is easy to prepare, it is inexpensive, it is beautiful to serve, and as an extra bonus, prepared early in the day it saves time for hiking. Make up after breakfast and bake for dinner.

10 slices bread—approximately	2 eggs
10 slices cheese	1¼ cups milk
2 tablespoons butter	¼ teaspoon salt
	¼ teaspoon garlic salt
	⅛ teaspoon pepper

Lay four whole bread slices and one slice cut in half to fit the bottom of a 9 inch x 13 inch baking pan. Lay four cheese slices and one slice cut in half on top of the bread. Lay the rest of the bread on top of the cheese and the remaining cheese on the bread. Mix the eggs, milk and seasonings together and pour over the bread and cheese. Cover and let stand in the refrigerator at least two hours. Bake in a 350° oven thirty to forty minutes until puffy and browned.

Layered Casserole
(serves 4)

½ lb. noodles—cooked	1 can cheddar cheese soup
1 large can asparagus—drained	1 large can white meat tuna—drained
	salt and pepper to taste

Layer in a casserole dish in the order given. Salt and pepper each layer. Cover and bake in a 325° oven thirty-five to forty-five minutes.

Variation: Add grated Swiss cheese on each layer and on the top.

Shrimp in Foil
(serves 4)

Four shrimp per person is ample if the shrimp are large. For medium shrimp, add two extra per person. For a backyard barbecue, make up the packets ahead of time and freeze them.

16 shrimp	¼ teaspoon seasoned salt
16 mushrooms—sliced	¼ teaspoon garlic salt
4 green onions—sliced	4 drops Worcestershire
4 teaspoons chili sauce	sauce—optional
4 teaspoons chopped parsley	⅓ cup melted butter

Shell, clean and devein shrimp. Lay four shrimp in each of four twelve inch squares of aluminum foil. Top with mushrooms and green onions. Divide the chili sauce, parsley, salt, garlic salt, Worcestershire and melted butter evenly between the four servings. Close foil to make a tightly sealed package. Grill five to ten minutes over charcoal or bake in a 400° oven twenty to twenty-five minutes.

Baked Tuna Potatoes
(serves 4)

Served with a salad or fruit dish, Baked Tuna Potatoes completes the evening meal.

4 very large baking potatoes	1 can tuna fish—drained
¼ cup chopped green onions	salt and pepper to taste
½ to ¾ cup milk	½ cup grated cheese
	¼ teaspoon paprika

Bake potatoes in a 375° oven for one hour or until done. Remove from the oven. Cut in half and scoop out the potato from each half, leaving the skin intact. Cream the potatoes with the onion, milk, tuna fish and salt and pepper. Add more or less milk to reach desired consistency. Fill the skins, piling the potato mixture high in the center. Top with grated cheese and sprinkle with paprika. Run back in the oven for ten to fifteen minutes.

Barbecued Ribs
(4 to 5 pounds)

Use either pork or beef ribs. These are best over an open fire or a charcoal fire. Some places will not allow open fires, and, in that case, you will have to bake them in the oven or over briquets. Place ribs on foil to avoid heavy cleanup.

4 to 5 lbs. ribs	3 tablespoons soy sauce
1 cup chicken broth—fresh or canned	½ teaspoon seasoned salt
	¼ teaspoon lemon pepper
2 tablespoons catsup	3 tablespoons barbecue
⅓ cup honey	sauce—commercial

Place ribs in a deep dish or pan. Mix the rest of the ingredients together and bring to a boil. Simmer five minutes. Pour over ribs and marinate overnight (or all day). Bake covered in a 300° oven one and a half hours. Uncover and bake thirty minutes to an hour longer.

If cooking over an open fire, watch and turn frequently.

Steaks Unusual

The simple steak and baked potato dinner is an all-round favorite. This recipe gives it a new twist.

4 to 6 steaks	½ cup sweet hot mustard
2 teaspoons coarse salt	½ cup honey

Pat steaks dry. Rub with salt. Mix the mustard and honey together and spread on both sides of the steaks. Let stand one hour at room temperature. Cook fast, five minutes on each side for a medium rare steak.

Mixed Grill

Use leftover fish, pork, beef, chicken or any combination you choose. Cut the leftovers into chunks approximately bite-size. Dip in batter and fry until golden.

Batter

1 cup pancake mix	1 egg
1 cup beer (or water)	salt and pepper to taste

Mix all ingredients together.
Variation: Dip and fry vegetables.

The All American Hot Dog

A summer without a hot dog is like a summer without sunshine! Here are a couple of different ways to enjoy them.

Swiss Swirls

The thicker the hot dog the better they work.

hot dogs	a slice bacon for each hot dog
strips of Swiss cheese	toasted hot dog buns—with butter

Split hot dog in half lengthwise, not quite all the way through the meat. Lay a strip of Swiss cheese one-fourth inch thick and the length of the hot dog down in the center. Close the hot dog around the cheese and wrap a strip of bacon around it spiral fashion. Secure with a toothpick. Broil the hot dogs or cook over the grill. Open the buns and generously butter them. Toast under the broiler or over a grill. When the bacon is crisp and the hot dog hot, place in toasted bun.
Variation: Use cheddar cheese.

Red Devils

10 to 12 weiners	⅛ teaspoon pepper
¼ cup butter	1½ tablespoons Worcester-
1 cup finely chopped onion	shire sauce
2 cloves garlic—minced	1½ tablespoons mustard
½ teaspoon salt	1½ teaspoons sugar
	½ cup chili sauce

Melt butter in a skillet. Add the onion and garlic and cook until tender, about ten minutes. Stir frequently. Add all other ingredients and simmer five minutes. Split the weiners lengthwise. Arrange them split side up in a shallow pan. Spoon the sauce over them. Run under the broiler until piping hot. Serve in hot dog buns. Pile on the extra sauce.

Crab Meat Delicious
(serves 4)

If you are in fresh crab country, use the fresh crab. If not use canned crab.

8 oz. crab—fresh or canned	1 can mushroom soup
4 hard-cooked eggs—grated	½ cup grated sharp cheddar
	cheese

Flake the crab meat. Grate the eggs in the bottom of a greased baking dish. Heat the mushroom soup and add the cheese and crab meat. Stir until blended. Pour over the eggs.

Bake in 350° oven twenty to twenty-five minutes until hot and bubbly.

Variation: Season with salt and pepper and garlic salt. Add a layer of Parmesan cheese on the top.

Zucchini Mexicana
(serves 6 to 8)

If you plan to serve a fewer number of people, divide the ingredients into two baking dishes instead of one. Freeze one to use at a later date. If you do not have a freezer, keep one or two days in the refrigerator and change the taste of the casserole by adding:

ground beef
shredded beef
chopped cooked chicken

You may also vary the amount of cheese used in the recipe. From a half to a full pound is acceptable.

½ cup rice—cooked
1 lb. jack cheese
1 can chili peppers (7 oz. size)
3 medium zucchini
1 large tomato
1 pint sour cream

2 tablespoons chopped green onions
2 tablespoons chopped green pepper
1 teaspoon garlic salt
1 teaspoon oregano
salt and pepper to taste
2 tablespoons parsley

Spread the cooked rice evenly over the bottom of a buttered two quart baking dish. Grate the cheese and spread half of it over the rice. Wash the chilies and remove seeds. Lay on the cheese. Slice the zucchini and spread evenly over the chilies. Slice the tomato in thin slices and layer on the zucchini. Mix sour cream, green onions, green peppers, garlic salt, salt and pepper to taste together and spread on the layered mixture. Sprinkle the rest of the grated cheese on top. Sprinkle parsley on the cheese. Bake in a 350° oven for thirty to forty minutes until browned and bubbly. Serve with warmed corn or flour tortillas and butter.

Note: When adding meat, layer between chilis and zucchini.

Fast French Pizza
(serves 4 to 6)

2 cups biscuit mix
2 tablespoons mustard
½ cup milk
2 cans tomato sauce
1 tablespoon sugar
1 tablespoon minced onion
½ teaspoon oregano
1 tablespoon mustard

¼ pound sausage—cooked and drained
½ cup sliced mushrooms—fresh or canned
1 cup grated mozzarella cheese
¼ cup grated Parmesan cheese—optional

Mix biscuit mix, mustard and milk in a bowl. Blend well. Knead one minute and roll to fit a baking sheet (pizza pan if you take one with you). Prick surface with the tines of a fork. Bake in a 425° oven for five minutes. Remove pizza dough and reduce heat to 375°. Prepare the filling. Heat tomato sauce, sugar, onion, oregano and mustard until bubbly. Spread out evenly on the dough. Sprinkle the sausage and mushrooms on the sauce. Top with the cheeses. Bake until browned, about fifteen to twenty minutes.

Variations: Add chopped green pepper, cooked ground beef, half cooked chopped bacon, or olives—black or green.

"THAR'S GOLD IN THEM THAR HILLS"

The province of British Columbia boasts a rich history of surefooted progress in the great Pacific Northwest. The awesome beauty of the Coastal Mountains, the rough and rugged shoreline along the vast Pacific Ocean, the fertile Okanagan Valley and the Rocky Mountain chain, provide ample evidence to the traveler. But above all, the Cariboo serves to stimulate the imagination, with its unique position in the proud history of the province.

A century ago fur traders, trappers and settlers braved the fast currents of the mighty Fraser River and took portage across the high, dry mountains and narrow plains into the Cariboo. Then gold took the fore as thousands upon thousands of fortune-seeking men raced into this great wilderness in search of the yellow mineral that would make some men rich and others old before their time.

And so it was. Men of every walk of life had their chance. Billy Barker, for whom the gold-mining town of Barkerville is named, made his fortune along the Cariboo, as did many others as they outsmarted nature's hiding places for the richest metal known to man.

The Cariboo thrived and flourished as mother earth gave up her bounty.

Suddenly it was over. The great gold strikes reduced in

number and the miners faded away, leaving the aftermath of their plunderous search to return to the natural state of existence before their invasion. So it is today.

Aging old buildings in countless ghost towns bear mute evidence of the tremendous prosperity that made the Cariboo a household word.

While traveling aimlessly through that historic country in our own search for adventure, we encountered a treasure still remaining in the vast wilderness of the Cariboo.

The treasure in this instance is more easily available than the plentiful gold of a century ago. No gold pan or shovel, sluice box or pick is required to uncover the precious bounty. The treasure is there in luxurious growth to simply reach out and pick casually from the low vines and stunted trees of the backcountry. The treasure is there for all to enjoy, the most delicious and nutritious harvest imaginable, in the form of tender, fat and juicy huckleberries, wild strawberries, bimbleberries, saskatoon and Indian Crawler berries. They are there in sumptuous quantities, submitting their destinies to the terrible winter cold, the summer's warmth and nature's erratic water supplies.

All along the old Cariboo Trail these vines and bushes fight for survival against the demands of hardier and larger vegetation, yet the delicate balance of nature provides their survival against difficult odds.

We left the main Highway 97 along the trail and struck off across the wooded stretches on the road to Likely, high in the interior mountains. The road was tedious but interesting. Our destination seemed constantly "just over the next hill," as we enjoyed the trip, leisurely stopping to enjoy the fruits of nature as we went.

The vast backcountry is heavily vegetated but sparsely populated. The trails of any consequence, through the fir timber growth, are made by bear, deer, elk and many of the smaller animals as they roam in search of the ample quantities of fruits, berries and soft meadow grasses. Even so, the supplies of these succulent berries are plentiful and within easy reach.

Reaching our destination of Likely we struck up an acquaintance with the "monarch of the Cariboo," Captain Norman Evans-Atkinson, a retired British Army officer. Captain Evans-Atkinson's hardy spirit and youthful gait scarcely provide credence to his age. His gold claim lies along the eastern banks of Cedar Creek, several miles from Likely, where he has placer mined continuously since filing his claim in 1929.

The Captain's hospitality included gold-panning near fresh diggings beside the creek and then a berry picking expedition along the overgrown, narrow paths near his simple miner's cabin.

He explained that he had enjoyed the sweet, wild huckleberries for over forty years, using them in a variety of simple dishes. He decided to thin the overgrowth surrounding the vines on several occasions, however later concluded that they seem to grow best in a somewhat crowded and natural state. With a twinkle in his eye, he suggested that his longevity was probably due to the many berry treats to be found there.

At his invitation we roamed through the heavy thickets, gathering many of the berries, realizing the value of picking our own fruits in their natural setting rather than tediously screening through the markets back home for similar berries which had been force-grown, fertilized, sprayed and later mauled on their way to the consumer.

We found great quantities of wild strawberries growing along the mossy banks of Plato Island, standing in picturesque isolation in the center of nearby Quesnel Lake. Captain Evans-Atkinson told us the story of "Plato John" Likely, for whom the village was named.

We listened with interest as he described the exploits of Plato John, who, during the height of the gold strikes of the area, would call together other miners camped near the fast-moving creek, to gather on the island. There in the peaceful solitude he read the works of Plato to the miners. Afterwards, in open forum, they would discuss their individual philosophies, then return to their crude cabins or tents to contemplate their singular place in humanity.

We sat entranced by the captain's stories of an era long past, sipping his Englishman's favorite, hot tea, from frail little china cups that somehow looked a bit out of place in his huge, rough hands.

Before taking our leave, the Captain urged us to investigate the open meadows near Quesnel Forks, the old ghost town some ten miles distant.

After reluctantly saying our goodbyes we headed through the dense fir groves toward the ghost town. The road was difficult and rarely traveled. At many points our son would get out and lift the thin saplings out of the road so we could pass.

Arriving at Quesnel Forks we stood in awe as we reflected on the history of the once heavily populated old town. The sparse wind whistled through the rafters of sagging old cottonwood log buildings. It was eerie but extraordinarily peaceful.

The huckleberry bushes described by the Captain were there, spreading out in every direction. We took our plastic cups in hand and gently took a generous supply for later use in pancakes. We also cooked down a simple syrup of raw sugar, into which we crushed the small, purplish berries.

The flavor was unique and quite unlike the blueberry syrups available in the markets back home.

Our stay in the ghost town was rewarded with other interesting items. We found the old buildings fascinating. On the walls of the largest and most structurally impressive building there, we were able to make out the dim lines of what appeared to be Chinese characters. This was the Chinese Masonic Hall, described earlier to us by Captain Evans-Atkinson. The low ceilings of the building, including the loft area seemed to verify its use by the extremely short

Chinese who were a dominant portion of the population of the once prosperous and busy town.

At the western edge of the cluster of buildings, the fast Quesnel River and the Cariboo River join in a mighty rush. Near the terminal of the two streams, the sagging wooden timbers of the old bridge continue to resist the constant stress of the churning water and provide a scenic reminder of the state of decay that so aptly describes Quesnel Forks.

The remainder of our stay there was given over to discovering the new found "treasure" of the Cariboo Country, the plentiful supplies of nature's gifts to all who will search for it.

In our estimation, "Thar's gold, in them thar hills." . . . It's the new gold of the Cariboo.

SOUP AND
SOUP STARTERS

Hot or cold, soup is a filler-upper. It can be a hearty chowder or a light bouillon. Drink it from a mug, sip it from a cup, eat it with a spoon but do include lots of it "on the go."

Never throw anything away, it might be a soup starter. A tablespoon of gravy or vegetable juices left in the pan are wonderful "add to's" or a great beginning for an entire pot.

Packages of dry soups in several different flavors can be used as soups, as seasonings for dips and a flavorful way to cook roasts. They take very little space in the cupboard. Add leftovers to a soup base and you have a chowder or stew that can become a meal in itself.

Canned soups take on a new twist when combined. Use two and three different soups blended together for new and delicious innovations. Use as a base for fondues, as a cream sauce or a casserole filler.

We really like soups and we always have a variety packed in the cubicle designed for "soups only." I truly believe that we could enjoy soups for a whole month and never tire of them. Soups are the handiest things to have on rainy days or busy days, quick to prepare and serve and the cleanup is minimal.

Clam Chowder
(serves 8)

We are partial to the New England style chowder. This is one of our favorites when we arrive late at a destination. We also enjoy steaming bowls in rainy weather. As a matter of fact, we enjoy it any time, any place.

3 cans Snow's clam chowder
1 small can minced clams
3 soup cans light cream

¼ cup butter
1 teaspoon chopped parsley
¼ teaspoon white pepper—
    optional

Heat all ingredients together in a large saucepan. Serve with oyster crackers or pink crackers (recipe on page 22).

Celery Chowder
(serves 4)

Many times when you purchase celery, the outside stalks are somewhat tough. Here is a marvelous way to use those less desirable stalks and the green tops.

6 cups water
4 outside stalks celery
1 bunch green tops
1 fairly large potato
½ medium onion
1 teaspoon celery salt—
    optional

½ teaspoon monosodium
    glutamate—optional
1 cup chicken stock
2 tablespoons flour
½ cup light cream
2 tablespoons butter
1 teaspoon chopped parsley

Heat water to simmer. Chop celery into one-half inch pieces and add to simmering water. Add celery tops. Cover and reduce heat. Simmer slowly for one hour. Remove celery tops. Chop potato and onion and add to hot liquid. Add celery salt and monosodium glutamate. Blend chicken stock, light cream and flour together until smooth and stir into mixture until well blended. Cook until thickened slightly. Remove from fire. Add butter and parsley. Stir and serve.

Onion Chowder
(serves 3 to 4)

½ lb. bacon
2 onions—chopped
1 #1 can small
  potatoes—cubed

2 cups water
2 cups evaporated milk
salt and pepper to taste

Cut bacon into small pieces. Brown bacon and onion in a large saucepan. Add potatoes and simmer ten minutes. Add water and milk. Remove from fire, season and serve.

Soup Stock

Save any liquid in which you have cooked meat or vegetables. Add any bones and any leftovers. The flavor rendered really enhances this stock. Simmer two to three hours or even overnight on very low heat. If you need more flavor add chicken or bouillon cubes. Strain and use as a base for soups, sauces or gravies. It is delicious, as is, served with toasted bread cubes.

Variations: Use it as the liquid when preparing meat loaf or ground beef patties.

Use it to poach mushrooms and then thicken the remaining liquid to make a gravy. Serve the mushrooms on toast with the gravy over the top.

Tomato Sherry
(serves 2—double recipe for 4)

1 small can condensed tomato
  soup (10¾ oz.)
½ soup can of water

¼ teaspoon basil
3 tablespoons sherry
1 tablespoon Parmesan cheese

Heat soup, water and basil until very hot. Add sherry and stir until blended. Serve and top each bowl with the cheese.

Curried Pea Soup
(serves 2—double recipe for 4)

1 tablespoon butter
1 teaspoon curry powder
1 can condensed green pea
   soup (10¾ oz.)

¾ soup can water
1 teaspoon instant minced
   onion
1 tablespoon bacon bits

Melt butter in a saucepan. Add curry powder and blend well. Add pea soup. Blend water and onion together and add to pea soup mixture. Heat until very hot. Serve in bowls. Sprinkle bacon bits on top of soup.

Chicken and Leek
(serves 6 to 8)

1 package dry cream of
   chicken soup mix
¼ cup butter

1 teaspoon dill weed
1 package dry cream of leek
   soup mix

Mix the two soup mix packages together according to directions. Add dill weed during last five minutes of cooking time. Remove from fire and stir in the butter until dissolved. Serve at once.

Variation: Add pieces of leftover chicken or potatoes or both.

Mushroom Soup
(serves 4)

1 can potato soup
1 can mushroom soup
1 soup can water

1 soup can evaporated milk
1 teaspoon chopped parsley
1 bouquet garni—optional

Heat all ingredients until just bubbly. Reduce heat, cover and simmer for ten minutes. If using bouquet garni, remove before serving.

Variations: Add a can of salmon. Add a can of mixed vegetables. Add leftover fish chunks. Add potatoes and mushrooms.

Fresh Mushroom Soup
(serves 4 to 6)

6 cups water	½ teaspoon garlic salt
1 lb. fresh mushrooms	½ teaspoon salt
2 beef bouillon cubes	¼ teaspoon seasoned pepper
	2 tablespoons butter

Heat water in a large saucepan. Wash mushrooms and cut in slices. Add to the hot water. Add beef bouillon cubes and stir until dissolved. Add garlic salt and salt and pepper. Cover and simmer on low heat for forty-five minutes. Add butter and serve.

Variation: If you prefer a creamy mushroom soup, substitute milk for two of the six cups water. Thicken with three tablespoons flour mixed with a little water before serving.

Potato Chowder
(serves 4 to 6)

This chowder can be served hot or cold depending on the weather and your taste.

3 cups frozen hash-brown potatoes	1 teaspoon lemon juice
	½ cup chopped carrots
1 cup chopped onions	¼ cup chopped green pepper
1 can chicken broth (10¾ oz.)	2 cups milk
1 teaspoon salt	1 teaspoon chopped basil
¼ teaspoon seasoned pepper	1 teaspoon chopped parsley

Mix potatoes, onions, chicken broth, salt, pepper and lemon juice in a large saucepan. Heat and simmer for twenty minutes. Add carrots and peppers. Cook until carrots and peppers are tender. Stir in milk and heat until hot but do not boil. *Note:* If serving chilled do not heat after adding the milk. Just chill. At serving time sprinkle with the chopped basil and parsley mixed together.

Pumpkin Soup
(serves 4 to 6)

This soup can also be served hot or cold depending on weather and preference. Dollops of sweetened whipped cream served floating on the top of each bowl of soup is a really elegant touch whether served hot or cold.

2 cups water
2 cups beef broth—fresh or canned
¼ teaspoon thyme
1 bay leaf—medium size

1 can pumpkin (1 lb. size)
1½ teaspoons seasoned salt
1 teaspoon curry powder
¼ teaspoon nutmeg

Combine water, beef broth, thyme and bay leaf in large saucepan. Cover and simmer over medium heat thirty minutes. Add pumpkin, seasoned salt, curry powder and nutmeg. Blend well and cook thirty minutes longer, stirring as needed to prevent sticking. Strain and serve. If serving chilled it is best cooled to room temperature and then placed in the refrigerator overnight.

Vegetable Chicken Chowder
(serves 4 to 6)

4 slices bacon
1 cup sliced mushrooms— canned or fresh
1 medium onion—chopped
1 teaspoon parsley
½ teaspoon monosodium glutamate—optional
1 can cream of celery soup (10¾ oz. size)

1 can chicken vegetable soup (10¾ oz. size)
1 soup can water
1 cup cooked chicken—diced
1 small can whole kernel corn
½ cup chopped tomatoes— fresh or canned
salt and pepper to taste

Cut bacon into small pieces and brown until crisp in a large saucepan. Remove bacon. Add mushrooms, onions, parsley and monosodium glutamate. Cook until mushrooms and onions are tender. Add the crisp bacon, soups, water, chicken, corn and tomatoes. Cook over low heat thirty minutes stirring as needed. Season with salt and pepper and serve.

Variations: Substitute beef vegetable soup for the chicken vegetable soup and one cup diced cooked beef for the one cup diced cooked chicken.

Fish Chowder
(serves 4 to 6)

Use any white fish available with good results. If the fishing is good, have this for sure. One pound of fish makes the chowder recipe but we've had this chowder when the fishermen only produced a half pound for us to work with.

¼ lb. bacon	1 can milk
1 cup sliced celery	1 lb. white fish—cut in inch
½ cup chopped onion	pieces (approximately)
½ cup chopped potato	1 medium bay leaf
½ cup chopped carrots	2 tablespoons butter
2 cans cream of potato soup	1 teaspoon chopped parsley

Cut the bacon into small pieces and brown in a large saucepan. Add celery, onion, potato and carrots. Cook until vegetables are tender. Add soup and milk and heat until bubbly. Add fish and bay leaf. Cook until fish is tender, about ten minutes should do it. Remove bay leaf. Add butter and parsley. Serve at once. Salt and pepper if desired but do taste first.

Cheese Soup
(serves 4 to 6)

Be sure to use a natural cheese in the recipe. The processed cheeses are good but not for this soup as they will not melt properly.

2 cups boiling water
1 tablespoon chopped chives
1 teaspoon salt
⅛ teaspoon seasoned pepper
¼ cup butter

¼ cup flour
2 cups milk
2 cups grated natural sharp
  cheddar cheese

Bring water to a boil. Add chives, salt and pepper. Cover and simmer ten minutes. In a separate pan, melt the butter. Blend in the flour until you have a smooth paste but do not brown. Gradually add milk, stirring until well blended. Add the cheese and stir until cheese is melted. Gradually add hot water mixture. Heat but do not boil.

Variation: Add potatoes, carrots, onion and celery to the boiling water and cook until tender. You now have a cheese chowder.

Avocado Soup

Another chilled or steaming hot soup. We prefer it chilled and it is so simple to prepare. The avocados used for this soup should be very ripe. If you need to ripen some in a hurry, put them in a brown paper bag and store in the cabinet away from any light overnight.

2 large ripe avocados
2 tablespoons fresh lemon juice
1 can chicken broth (13¾ oz.
  size)
½ teaspoon salt

1 teaspoon grated onion
⅛ teaspoon seasoned pepper
1 teaspoon chopped chives
1½ cups light cream
paprika for garnish

Peel and remove pits from avocados. Cut into small pieces and put in a bowl. Sprinkle lemon juice over the pieces. Mash with a fork or the back of a spoon until a smooth mixture. Add chicken broth, salt, grated onion, seasoned pepper and chives. Blend until well mixed. Gradually stir in the cream until smooth. Chill two hours before serving. Sprinkle paprika on top of each bowl.

Shrimp Soup
(serves 4)

¼ cup butter
½ lb. baby shrimp—fresh or canned
¼ teaspoon garlic salt
¼ teaspoon parsley

¼ teaspoon dill weed
¼ teaspoon basil
⅛ teaspoon seasoned pepper
5 cups milk
2 tablespoons flour

Melt butter in a large saucepan. Add the shrimp and stir to coat evenly. Add garlic salt, parsley, dill weed, basil and seasoned pepper. Cook, stirring constantly, five minutes. Gradually add milk. Thicken with flour mixed with a little of the cold milk. Heat but do not boil.

Chinese Egg Drop
(serves 2–double recipe for 4)

1 can chicken broth (13¾ oz size)
2 tablespoons chopped green onions
⅛ teaspoon garlic salt

⅛ teaspoon monosodium glutamate—optional
1 egg
crisp Chinese noodles—optional

Heat chicken broth, green onions, garlic salt and monosodium glutamate until it begins to bubble. Break egg into a cup and stir quickly with a fork. Drop egg into soup and stir vigorously for thirty seconds. Pour into bowls and serve with crisp noodles dropped into the soup or eaten on the side.

French Onion Soup
(serves 4)

2 large onions
¼ cup butter
4 cups boiling water

2 beef bouillon cubes
4 slices toast
1 tablespoon Parmesan cheese

Slice onions crosswise as thin as possible. Melt butter in a large saucepan and add the onions. Cook until transparent but do not brown. Cover with boiling water and add beef cubes. Gently stir until bouillon is dissolved. Cover and simmer slowly for thirty minutes. Meanwhile sprinkle the Parmesan cheese evenly over the toast. Pour the soup into bowls. Trim the toast so that each slice may be floated on top of the soup.

Black Bean Soup
(serves 4 to 6)

The only reminder you need is not to forget to soak the beans overnight.

2 cups black beans	2 tablespoons flour
1½ quarts water—	1 teaspoon salt
approximately	¼ teaspoon paprika
1 quart chicken stock	2 cups milk
½ cup chopped onions	4 tablespoons sherry
½ cup chopped celery	2 hard cooked eggs—grated
¼ cup chopped carrots	4 thin slices lemon
3 tablespoons butter	

Soak the beans in water overnight. Drain off the water. Put the drained beans in a large saucepan. Add the chicken stock, onions, celery and carrots. Cover and simmer one and a half hours. Strain the soup using the back of a spoon to mash as much through as possible. Melt the butter in a saucepan. Blend the flour into the melted butter until a smooth paste. Add the salt and paprika. Gradually add the milk. Pour the milk mixture into the strained bean mixture and blend until smooth. Heat until very hot. When ready to serve, add the sherry. Pour into bowls. Garnish each with the grated egg and a lemon slice.

A creative project by the side of a stream. A good "do ahead—take along" project. Take your pick.

Tomato Supreme
(serves 2 to 4)

When you find fresh tomatoes try this soup. We've used large red ones and small cherry tomatoes with equal success. Canned tomatoes still make a delicious soup so don't hesitate to try this recipe if you are out of fresh tomatoes.

2½ cups tomatoes	2 tablespoons flour
¼ cup chopped onion	2 cups beef bouillon
½ cup chopped celery—can	½ teaspoon sugar
use tops and leaves	½ teaspoon paprika
2 tablespoons butter	¼ teaspoon basil
	salt and pepper to taste

Cut the tomatoes into pieces. Put in a large saucepan with onion and celery. Cook for twenty to thirty minutes, stirring as needed to prevent scorching. Add a little water if necessary. Strain and mash through a sieve. Discard pulp, seeds and skins. Melt the butter and blend in the flour until smooth. Pour in the beef bouillon and stir until well blended. Add the strained tomato mixture and the seasonings. Heat until thickened slightly and very hot. Serve at once.

Lobster Bisque
(serves 2 to 4)

This recipe is given for lobster, but salmon, crab or shrimp may be substituted.

1 can asparagus soup	½ to 1 cup lobster
1 can mushroom soup	½ teaspoon lemon juice
1½ cups cream	¼ cup white wine—optional
	seasoned salt and pepper

Do not add any water to soups. Combine soups with cream. Add lobster meat and lemon juice. Heat until bubbling. Add wine and seasonings.

Variation: Delete cream and heat. Serve over rice as a main dish.

Vegetable Cream
(serves 4 to 6)

We adapted this delight after enjoying a similar version aboard a magnificent Greek cruise ship, the *Stella Solaris,* flagship of the Sun Line. This was served one evening after we had returned to the comfort of this beautiful vessel after a day ashore in Cartagena, Colombia, South America.

The chef showed us how to combine the ingredients to achieve a most satisfactory vegetable cream soup.

It can be prepared with leftover vegetables in the camper. We use cauliflower, broccoli, spinach, carrots or whatever we have left over. The basic recipe adapts to any of those.

1 can cream of chicken soup
1 can celery soup
1 cup leftover vegetables—
  cooked
1 tablespoon butter

1 cup milk
¼ teaspoon monosodium
  glutamate—optional
⅛ teaspoon nutmeg
salt and pepper to taste

Combine the soups and blend well. Mash the vegetables as much as possible. Blend into the soup mixture. Add butter, milk and seasonings. Heat until very hot, stirring to prevent sticking. Serve plain or with croutons.

French Fried Onion Soup
(serves 4 to 6)

Use as a soup or as a side dish with lunch or dinner.

2 cans cream of onion soup
1 can milk
1 teaspoon parsley

¼ teaspoon seasoned salt
¼ teaspoon onion salt
1 can French fried onion rings

Blend the soup and milk together in a saucepan. Add the seasonings and heat thoroughly. Chop the French fried onion rings and divide evenly in the serving bowls. Pour the hot soup over the onion rings and serve immediately.

Things to Add

To any canned soup or homemade soup stock add:

leftover meat—cut in small
  pieces
leftover vegetables
leftover gravy
leftover meat juices
leftover vegetable juices

bacon bits
cheese
croutons
noodles
rice
mushrooms
extra herbs and spices

SALADS AND DRESSINGS

Salads have crept into a position of honor in the American household and they are a blessing. Most salads are simple to prepare, nutritious in many ways and certainly taste-satisfying to most of us.

Salad preparation on the go need not suffer. Lettuce and good salad greens are available everywhere and welcome at every table. There are a number of salads which do adapt themselves very easily to travel and those favorites of ours are included.

Since the majority of vacation travel and camper excursions occur during the principal growing season, there are numerous salad ingredients available most of the time. Fresh lettuce is never more delicious than when bought from rural sources. Fresh, tender green onions, vine-ripened tomatoes, cucumbers and the like seem always to be in abundance when we travel and therefore become a companionable part of our travel salads.

As for dressings, many can be made up in minutes with oil, vinegar, water and seasoning packets which may be dry-stored in the vehicle at all times. If the family favorites are available, a good salad can be produced in less time than it takes to make a decision about which dressing to use.

Several of the following salads and dressings were developed on the occasion of discovering we were temporarily out of one or more ingredients of a particular favorite. Necessity *is* the mother of invention.

When all else fails, remember that the literal definition of a salad is, "any combination of greens and accompanying dressing."

Salads and Their Dressings

Overnight Dressing

2 tablespoons vinegar	½ teaspoon mustard
1 tablespoon oil	¼ teaspoon cracked pepper
2 teaspoons sugar	¼ teaspoon seasoned pepper

Cover and soak in the refrigerator overnight. Strain and serve over tossed salad greens. Use to marinate sliced tomatoes, cucumbers, onions, green peppers or a combination of any raw vegetable.

Honey Salad Dressing
(makes approximately 2 cups)

1 teaspoon paprika	⅓ cup honey
½ teaspoon dry mustard	3 tablespoons lemon juice
½ teaspoon salt	1 cup salad oil
½ teaspoon celery salt	¼ cup vinegar

Mix dry ingredients. Add honey, lemon juice and vinegar. Add oil and beat with a fork until blended. Store in the refrigerator until ready to use.

Red and Green Salad

sliced red onions	shredded lettuce
sliced tomatoes	Honey Salad Dressing

Marinate sliced onions and tomatoes in dressing for at least two hours. Add shredded lettuce and toss.

Seafood Louie Dressing
(makes approximately 1½ cups)

1 cup mayonnaise
½ cup chili sauce
2 tablespoons lemon juice

1 teaspoon Worcestershire
  sauce
1 tablespoon minced chives
½ teaspoon dill weed

Mix all ingredients together and store in the refrigerator until ready to use.

Salad Louie

Use shrimp, crab or lobster in a Louie Salad. You may use any combination of two or three seafoods.

Served with French bread and white wine, this Louie becomes a meal fit for a king. A-La-King-Louie!

shredded lettuce
tomato wedges
quartered hard-cooked eggs

pieces of cooked seafood—
  crab, lobster or shrimp
Seafood Louie Dressing

Arrange on individual plates or one large salad bowl the ingredients in the order given. Serve the dressing drizzled over the top or on the side, letting each person serve their own dressing.

Garlic Salad Dressing
(makes approximately ¾ cup)

¼ cup white vinegar
1 teaspoon dry mustard
½ clove garlic—minced

⅔ cup olive oil—or salad oil
1 teaspoon salt
¼ teaspoon pepper
2 tablespoon sugar

Layered Vegetable Salad
(serves 4 to 6)

This salad gives you a lot of leeway. It is made ahead of time, but the amount of time ahead is up to you. Make the night before, early in the day you plan to serve the salad, or two hours before serving.

1½ pounds medium potatoes
salt to taste
pepper to taste
1 medium green pepper—
   sliced in thin rings

1 cucumber—peeled and
   thinly sliced
1 medium red onion—sliced
   thin in rings
2 tablespoons finely chopped
   parsley

Boil potatoes in salted water until tender. Drain, cool, peel and thinly slice. Arrange potato slices in the bottom of a deep bowl. Sprinkle with salt and pepper to taste. Arrange the rest of the ingredients in the order given. Pour one recipe Garlic Salad Dressing over all. Cover and chill until ready to serve. Baste once or twice by tilting the bowl and turning it around or by using a baster or a ladle.

Wilted Spinach with Mushrooms
(serves 4 to 6)

1 lb. spinach—young and
   tender leaves
¼ lb. mushrooms—canned or
   fresh
4 slices bacon
¼ cup vinegar
½ teaspoon salt

1 clove garlic—minced
¼ teaspoon pepper
¼ teaspoon oregano
¼ teaspoon basil
½ teaspoon sugar
½ teaspoon dry mustard

Wash spinach and drain. Tear off leaves and break into edible pieces. Clean and wipe the mushrooms dry. Slice and add to the spinach. Fry bacon until crisp. Drain and crumble; set aside. Combine vinegar, salt, garlic, pepper, oregano, basil, sugar and dry mustard. Reheat the bacon drippings. Pour in the vinegar mixture slowly, stirring constantly. Pour hot dressing over spinach and mushrooms. Add crumbled bacon, toss and serve.

Farmer's Salad

cherry tomatoes—cut in half
green onions—sliced ¼" thick

cucumber—peeled and
    chopped
blue cheese dressing—bottled

Mix tomatoes, onions and cucumbers together. Add to each serving one teaspoon bottled blue cheese dressing. Stir until mixed. Let stand ten minutes to improve the flavors. Stir again just before serving.

German Carrot Salad
(serves 4 to 6)

4 carrots
3 medium apples

2 tablespoons honey
2 tablespoons lemon juice

Wash and scrape carrots. Peel apples. Grate the carrots and apples into a bowl. Mix with honey and lemon juice. Stir until well blended. Chill one hour before serving.
Variation: Serve with beets, or stuff tomatoes.

Jello Salads

Make any gelatin salad that you make at home. A word of caution however. Be sure it has set before driving. If refrigerator space is crowded, put the Jello salad in a tightly covered container and submerge in a cold mountain stream to set it.

We have found that we do not use as many Jello salads as we do at home. We are constantly on the move and never know when we plan to "move on." Also we need our space in the refrigerator. We do make Jello on occasion for dessert.

111

Cold Green Beans
(serves 4)

¼ cup sugar
½ cup vinegar
2 tablespoons water
1 tablespoon salad oil

1 package dry French dressing
1 large can whole green beans
1 medium red onion—sliced
  thin

Mix sugar, vinegar, water, oil and French dressing together. Bring to a boil. Turn off heat. Layer green beans and sliced onions in a deep dish. Pour the hot mixture over all. Let stand at room temperature for one hour, then chill in the refrigerator for twenty-four hours before serving. Store in container with tight-fitting lid.

Variation: Use mushrooms instead of green beans.

Fruit Salad

One:
orange sections
grapefruit sections

sliced avocado
French dressing

Buy orange and grapefruit sections canned or in jars in the dairy section of the market. Add avocado slices and top with dressing.

Two:
apple slices
1 can mixed fruit—with juices

1 teaspoon lemon juice
1 teaspoon honey

Mix all together and chill before serving.

Three:
sliced bananas
1 teaspoon lemon juice
1 small can green grapes—or
  fresh equivalent

1 small can pineapple
  chunks—drained

Slice bananas and add lemon juice to prevent them from turning brown. Add rest of ingredients and serve in bowls. Be sure to save the juices for fruit drinks.

Colorful Compote

1 small can kidney beans—
  drained
1 avocado—sliced
½ green pepper—chopped fine

½ onion—chopped fine
2 hard cooked eggs—chopped
  fine
salt and pepper to taste
1 tablespoon salad oil

Mix all ingredients together and serve on a lettuce leaf. Serve at room temperature or well chilled.

VEGETABLES

Notwithstanding the fact that we all need vegetables as a part of our general nutrition every day, it is good to consider just how downright delicious they can be whether at home or on the go.

All of us have our favorites and those are the ones we should concentrate on, especially when we travel. Very often small children resist them, but by careful preparation and painstaking persuasion, even the most finicky can be converted. Most vegetable lovers are avid devotees for life.

We too have our favorites and we have them often. We prefer fresh vegetables to frozen or canned varieties. We consider frozen vegetables generally out of the question while traveling in our camper, for freezer space is very restricted and too valuable for other things. We take along canned varieties as a reasonable compromise. The thing we enjoy most is to find certain wild vegetables along the way and have them as fresh as is possible. Often we will find small produce stalls along country roads which boast vine-ripened items at their peak of flavor and nutrition. (Look under the heading "Along The Side of The Road" for examples.)

As for nutrition, there are special demands on our systems while traveling, and vegetables, as a part of our travel cuisine, can supply much-needed vitamins and minerals as

114

well as carotene and chlorophyll. This is especially important for growing children. Vegetables are an important and necessary part of food on the go. Some of our favored techniques will fill the bill.

Barbecued Onions

1 onion per person—sliced
2 tablespoons barbecue
  sauce—prepared

1 teaspoon butter
1 tablespoon honey
salt and pepper to taste

Make up individual packets and store in the refrigerator until ready to use. Lay sliced onions in the center of a square of aluminum foil. Add rest of ingredients in the order given. Fold edges and seal package tightly. Cook over coals, turning often or bake in a 325° oven thirty-five to forty minutes.

Vegetables in Foil

For each person you will need the following:

¼ onion—chopped
½ tomato—sliced
1 small zucchini—sliced

1 piece celery—sliced diagonally
1 teaspoon butter
salt and pepper to taste

Layer in the order given in the center of a square of aluminum foil. Seal the edges. Cook fifteen to twenty minutes on top of coals or bake in a 325° oven twenty to thirty minutes.

Best Baked Beans

1 large can baked beans
1 onion—chopped fine
¼ cup catsup
1 tablespoon mustard

3 tablespoons honey or molasses
4 slices bacon—cut into small
  pieces

Mix all ingredients together. Bake in a 350° oven forty minutes or cook in pan on top of stove over low heat, stirring often to prevent sticking.

Scalloped Potatoes

Allow the following ingredients for each person. Pack in individual foil packets or bake in a baking dish or cook very slow on top of the stove, covered.

1 medium potato—sliced thin	**1 teaspoon flour**
1 small onion—sliced thin	**salt and pepper to taste**
2 teaspoons butter	**2 tablespoons milk**

Layer potato, onion, butter, flour, salt and pepper. Pour milk over all and fold over edges of foil into a tight wrap.

Brown Rice for Four

Try serving brown rice instead of white rice for a change. Cut recipe in half for two.

3 cups water	**½ teaspoon salt**
1 tablespoon oil	**1 cup brown rice**

Bring water to a boil. Add oil and salt. Stir in the rice. When it comes to a boil, stir and cover. Reduce heat to a very low simmer. Cook forty minutes or until all water is absorbed. The rice should be light and fluffy. Check often because overcooking will cause the rice to become gummy.

Roasted Corn I

Allow one dozen ears for four people. Open the corn and remove the silks. Close husks. Tie the open end with a piece of string. Soak ears in water for five minutes. Remove from water and drain for one minute. Lay on a grill several inches above coals or bake in 350° oven. The coals will take approximately twenty to twenty-five minutes, the oven method will take approximately thirty minutes. The absorbed water turns to steam and makes the corn juicy and tender.

Roasted Corn II

This method is especially appealing because you make it at home or early in the day and cook whenever you please.

12 ears of corn	salt and pepper
12 teaspoons butter	12 squares of foil to fit corn

Shuck and clean the corn. Rinse in cold water to remove all traces of the silks. Lay each ear of corn in a square of foil. Put butter on top and sprinkle with salt and pepper. Fold the foil over the corn lengthwise with a drug store wrap (that is a double fold). Fold the ends over twice to seal securely. Store in the refrigerator until ready to use. Bake in the oven thirty minutes or over coals twenty to twenty-five minutes.

Marvelous Medley
(serves 4 to 6)

1 small can lima beans	1 small can artichoke hearts
1 small can button mushrooms	1 small can little white onions
1 small can French cut green beans	1 slice bacon—crisp and crumbled

Make in a saucepan, bake in the oven or prepare individual foil packets. Drain the vegetables, Layer all together and season as you choose. Top with bacon, crumbled. Heat until hot and bubbly.

Onion Pilaff
(serves 6 to 8)

2 tablespoons butter
1 package onion soup mix

3 cups water or chicken broth
or half and half of each of
the above
1½ cups rice—white or brown

Melt the butter in a heavy skillet or saucepan. Add the soup mix and water or broth. Stir in the rice and bring to a boil. Stir as needed and cook twenty to thirty minutes or until all water is absorbed. Especially good with poultry and fish.

Sauerkraut
(serves 4)

1 large can sauerkraut
2 tablespoons bacon drippings

salt and pepper
8 wieners or 4 knockwurst

Rinse sauerkraut in cold water and drain well. Melt bacon drippings in skillet. Add sauerkraut and season with salt and pepper. Lay weiners or knockwurst on top. Cover and simmer over low heat thirty to thirty-five minutes. The kraut and the weiners will steam until hot and tender.

Succotash
(serves 4)

Early settlers learned this from the Indians. In the pioneer spirit,, combine the following:

1 can lima beans
1 can corn
¾ cup milk

1 tablespoon sugar
1 tablespoon butter or drippings
salt and pepper to taste

Mix ingredients together and simmer slowly for twenty to twenty-five minutes.

Stewed Tomatoes
(serves 3 to 4)

1 #2 can tomatoes	¼ teaspoon monosodium
2 tablespoons sugar	glutamate—optional
3 tablespoons butter	salt and pepper to taste
½ teaspoon onion salt	2 tablespoons flour
	¼ cup water

Bring to a boil all but the flour and water. Thicken with the flour and water mixed together into a paste. Stir and cook until thickened. Serve in bowls with the juices.

Poached Mushrooms
(serves 4 to 6)

We usually make these once a week. The leftover mushrooms can be stored in the refrigerator and added to any number of dishes. The leftover juice can be thickened and served as soup.

1 pound fresh mushrooms	⅛ teaspoon pepper
1 tablespoon butter	½ teaspoon freeze-dried shal-
2 cups water	lots
½ teaspoon salt	½ teaspoon chopped parsley
	½ teaspoon freeze-dried chives

Wash and clean the mushrooms. Poach them whole or sliced or chopped. Add all other ingredients. Bring to a boil. Reduce heat and cover tightly. Simmer ten minutes. Drain and use or store in the refrigerator and use as needed.

For Soup

Add 1 cup milk or cream
¼ cup of the poached mushrooms
flour to thicken

Top with Parmesan cheese when serving.

119

Spanish Rice
(serves 3 to 4)

Spanish rice may be used as a side dish or, with additions, an evening meal casserole. The variations are limitless. Some of the things to add are meat, chicken, sausage, shredded beef and cheese. Stuff green peppers, fish or pork chops.

2 onions—chopped	1 can tomato soup
4 strips bacon—cut in pieces	¼ cup water
1 cup rice	salt and pepper to taste

Sauté the onions and bacon until bacon is done. Add rice and stir to blend. Add tomato soup and water. Cover and cook thirty to forty minutes or until light and fluffy and moisture is absorbed. Season with salt and pepper and serve. It may also be baked in a 325° oven for the same length of time.

Luscious Mashed Potatoes
(serves 2 to 4)

2 cups mashed potatoes—packaged mix or fresh	½ cup grated Swiss cheese
	¼ teaspoon paprika
	¼ teaspoon garlic salt
2 tablespoons butter	¼ teaspoon lemon pepper
½ cup grated cheddar cheese	

Put half of the potatoes in a buttered casserole dish or skillet. Add half of the butter and the cheddar cheese. Add rest of the potatoes, rest of butter and Swiss cheese. Mix seasonings together and sprinkle on top. Bake in the oven twenty minutes, or cover with foil and cook over low heat until cheese is melted and mixture is hot.

Bacon Baked Potato

1 baking potato—per person
1 slice bacon—per person
salt and pepper to taste

Wash each potato and pat dry. Cut in half. Salt and pepper each side. Lay the slice of bacon in the center, folding ends to make fit. Close potato halves and wrap in foil. Bake until soft when squeezed between your fingers. Takes fifty minutes to one hour, whether you are baking in a 350° oven or an open fire.

Creamy Cabbage
(serves 4 to 6)

1 head cabbage—
  approximately 1 lb.
3 slices bacon—cut in pieces
1 medium onion—sliced thin
2 tablespoons butter

3 tablespoons flour
1 cup milk
salt and pepper to taste
⅛ teaspoon nutmeg
3 tablespoons heavy
  cream—or sour cream

Slice the cabbage into shreds. Cook in boiling salted water for five minutes. Drain. Sauté bacon and onion in heavy skillet for two minutes. Add butter and flour and blend well. Stir in milk gradually and stir to make a thickened sauce. Add seasonings and cabbage. Simmer slowly for ten minutes, stirring as needed. Just before serving stir in the cream or sour cream.

Excellent served with ham or Canadian bacon.

If the season is right, you may be able to buy fresh cabbages from farm stalls on the back roads.

BREADS

Man cannot live by bread alone, he also needs a little butter to spread on it. Taken a step further, a little jelly or jam doesn't hurt either.

The bakeries in the world come in all sizes. Many hotels and restaurants make their own breads, rolls and pastries. There is something about the aroma of freshly baked bread that will lead you directly to a one room bakery in the rural area of a small town.

On one memorable occasion, we were driving through the apple country. Each farmhouse had its own specialty. A map to guide us was acquired in the center of town. We were led on a tour of pies, jellies, jams, butters, cakes and ciders through the reds, oranges and greens of the apple lanes and byways.

Suddenly our senses told us that there was something wonderful happening somewhere—but where? Never before or since have I smelled such a captivating blend of spices floating through the air. We literally followed the aroma like Hansel and Gretel in the forest. Soon we were in a somewhat mild traffic jam for every car, camper, trailer and motor home had picked up the scent.

We arrived at a large apple sorting plant where they were packing apples for shipment. At one end of the open platform lines were forming. A housewife had come up with an idea for helping her husband use the apples sorted out from the shipping process. Every year she baked and sold apple cider doughnuts.

The whole family was involved because over the years filling the requests for these delicious doughnuts became a mountainous undertaking. The minute the first batch was plunged into the bubbling deep fat, the news was out. The lines formed and the lines did not stop until the announcement came—"No more till next season."

Apple Cider Doughnuts

On two of our trips to Canada we traveled in a large motor home complete with refrigerator with a full size freezer. These doughnuts take a bit of time but they freeze well. When traveling in our present mini-home, we make them up at home and take them along for the first two to three days.

3 eggs	2 teaspoons baking powder
1 cup sugar	1 teaspoon baking soda
2 tablespoons soft butter	1 teaspoon salt
⅓ cup apple cider	¾ teaspoon nutmeg
⅓ cup buttermilk	oil for deep frying
3¾ cups sifted flour	

Beat the eggs, sugar and butter in a mixer at high speed for two minutes. If using a rotary beater, take turns. Gradually blend in the apple cider and buttermilk at low speed on the mixer. Sift the flour, baking powder, baking soda, salt and nutmeg together. Add gradually and blend well. Cover and let stand in the refrigerator about one hour. Roll one-third of an inch thick and cut out doughnuts with a cutter. When all are cut, let rest ten minutes. Heat oil to 375° and fry three minutes, turning once, one and a half minutes on each side. Frost while warm.

Frosting

5 cups confectioner's sugar
1 teaspoon cinnamon

¼ teaspoon nutmeg
½ cup apple cider
1 teaspoon vanilla

Put sugar, cinnamon and nutmeg in a bowl. Add cider and vanilla and stir until creamy. While doughnuts are warm, dunk one side. Lay on waxed paper frosting side up to cool. The frosting will run down the sides to coat them.

Variations: Dip into coconut, chopped nuts or melted chocolate after frosting.

French Bread

This is the easiest recipe for French bread that I have ever used. If you have a mixer with a dough hook, and they are becoming very popular, it is pure child's play. For our own convenience we keep several loaves in the freezer. It is also a good way to get a teenager to help prepare for the upcoming trip.

1 package dry yeast—or 1
   fresh cake
1 cup lukewarm water
2 tablespoons sugar

1½ teaspoons salt
2 tablespoons melted shortening
3¾ cups flour

Mix yeast and warm water in a bowl until yeast is dissolved. Add sugar, salt and melted shortening. Sift flour and add very gradually until dough forms a ball and begins to come away from the sides of the bowl. Knead until elastic. If your mixer has a dough hook this is done very quickly and "look Ma, no hands." Place in a well greased bowl, turning once so top of dough is greased. Put bowl in warm water and cover. Let rise until double in bulk. Knead down and shape into long loaves on a baking sheet. Brush with cold water and slash diagonally across the tops three times / / / with a very sharp knife or a razor blade. Let rise until double in bulk. Bake in a 375° oven thirty to thirty-five minutes.

Ways to Enjoy

The first choice is warm from the oven with butter.

Slice a loaf in one inch thick slices. Butter and sprinkle each side with garlic salt. Shape the loaf back together and wrap in foil. Heat in oven and serve.

Pulled Herb Bread can be made by tearing a loaf of French bread into small uneven pieces. Melt a half cup butter in a large saucepan and add one-fourth cup finely chopped chives and one teaspoon herb seasoning. Dip the bread chunks into this mixture and toss until evenly coated. Lay on a baking sheet and run under the broiler. Turn frequently to permit even browning. Great with soups and salads.

Do try this unusual spread for French bread. Mix well,

> **¼ cup Italian salad dressing**
> **¼ cup butter**
> **¼ cup Parmesan cheese**

Spread on bread cut diagonally but not all the way through. Wrap in foil and bake in 375° oven ten to fifteen minutes.

If you do not wish to undergo the making of French bread, buy an already baked loaf at a bakery or market and try all the delightful ways to enjoy it.

Cheese Rounds

Serve with soup or salad in place of sandwiches. These also come in handy as snacks and hors d'oeuvres.

½ pound sharp cheddar cheese	**1 teaspoon paprika**
½ cup butter	**2 cups flour**

Grate cheese and cut butter into small pieces. Add paprika and sift in the flour. Use only enough flour to make a dough you can roll. Roll out one-fourth inch thick and cut out with a biscuit cutter or glass. You may find it easier to work with if chilled before rolling. Bake in a 350° oven eight to ten minutes.

Corn Lace Puffs

A delicate delicacy to add to any meal. The taste of sweet unsalted butter seems to add to the lightness of the puffs.

½ cup boiling water
½ cup white cornmeal

½ teaspoon salt
2 egg whites

Pour a half cup boiling water over the cornmeal mixed with a half teaspoon salt. Mix well and cool. Fold in the egg whites beaten stiff but moist. Drop batter by teaspoons onto a buttered baking sheet. Bake in a 350° oven twenty-five to thirty minutes until puffed and lightly browned. Serve with plenty of cold sweet butter.

Herb Dumplings

Use in any simmering liquid. Good in stews and chicken dishes. A great addition to any soup.

2 cups biscuit mix
1 egg—well beaten
⅔ cup milk
1 tablespoon chopped parsley

2 teaspoons grated onion
½ cup packaged croutons
1 teaspoon poultry seasoning

Combine all ingredients and blend well. All flour should be moistened. Drop by spoonfuls into any simmering liquid.

Blue Cheese Biscuits
(paradise in a pan)

These can be made with biscuits "from scratch" or packaged refrigerator biscuits.

12 biscuits—unbaked
½ cup melted butter
¼ cup crumbled blue cheese

Lay the biscuits in an 8 × 8 inch cake pan. Sides should be touching. Mix the butter and crumbled blue cheese together and pour evenly over the top of the biscuits. Bake in a 375° oven ten to twelve minutes until biscuits are puffed and brown. Test with a toothpick to make sure the centers are not soggy. Eat "as is."

Banana Bread

One recipe will make a loaf of bread or one to one and a half dozen muffins. The batter keeps well in the refrigerator and the finished product freezes well. You can use very ripe bananas with success.

⅔ cup sugar	1 teaspoon salt
½ cup butter	1 teaspoon baking soda
2 eggs	3 ripe bananas—mashed
2 cups flour	⅔ cup pecans—optional

Cream butter and sugar and add eggs one at a time. Sift flour, salt and baking soda together and blend into creamed mixture. Add bananas and nuts and blend well. Chill at least two hours before using, overnight is OK too. Bake in a greased loaf pan in a 375° oven thirty-five to forty minutes until a toothpick comes out clean when inserted. Bake in muffin tins, filled two-thirds full, in a 375° oven twenty minutes. Batter keeps a week or so in the refrigerator.

Mexican Corn Bread

This delicious and filling bread served with a salad qualifies as a meal.

1 cup yellow cornmeal	1 can cream style corn—1 lb. size
1 tablespoon chili powder	
½ teaspoon baking soda	1 lb. ground beef
¾ teaspoon salt	1 large onion—chopped
2 eggs—well beaten	1 large green pepper— chopped
1 cup milk	
¼ cup bacon drippings	½ lb. jack cheese—grated

Mix cornmeal, chili powder, baking soda, salt, eggs, milk, bacon drippings and corn together until well blended. Brown ground beef, drain and set aside. Grease a large cast iron skillet or a 9 inch x 13 inch baking pan. Pour in half of the batter. Sprinkle the ground beef, onion, pepper and cheese in layers, one at a time. Pour the remaining batter over the top. Bake in a 350° oven for one hour. Cut in squares to serve.

Hush Puppies

When we go trout fishing in the high mountains, we take the hush puppy ingredients for luck. So far, we have always had trout to serve them with.

¾ cup cornmeal	1 egg
¼ cup flour	⅓ cup milk
1 tablespoon baking powder	1 cup chopped green onions
¼ teaspoon salt	oil for frying

At home, mix the cornmeal, flour, baking powder and salt together and store in airtight plastic container. When ready to serve at the campsite, add the egg, milk and the green onions. Drop by spoonfuls into about one to two inches hot oil. Turn once.

Bran Muffins

The leftover muffins are excellent when split and spread with butter, then toasted for breakfast.

1½ cups bran flakes	1 cup flour
¼ cup shortening	2½ teaspoons baking powder
1 egg	¼ cup sugar
⅔ cup milk	½ teaspoon salt

Mix the bran flakes, shortening, egg and milk together. Sift the flour, baking powder, sugar and salt together and add to the first mixture. Blend well. Fill greased muffin tins two-thirds full and bake in a 400° oven fifteen to twenty minutes. Makes about a dozen. Sometimes we make a double recipe planned for toasting at breakfast.

Just Plain Corn Bread

Use as a bread to accompany a meal or use as a base for creamed chicken or creamed tuna. If you have a corn pone (or stick) pan at home, this batter makes them perfect every time. We don't take our heavy pan traveling for obvious reasons, it's heavy and filling them is time consuming. We usually bake the corn bread in a cast iron skillet. One skillet can be used for many things and the corn pone pan has one function only.

1 cup yellow cornmeal
1 cup white cornmeal
1 tablespoon sugar
1 teaspoon baking powder
½ teaspoon baking soda
½ teaspoon salt
1 tablespoon bacon drippings
1 cup buttermilk
1 egg—slightly beaten

Blend all the ingredients together until blended. Do not beat. Grease a cast iron skillet well and put in oven until very hot. Remove and pour in the batter. Bake in 400° oven twenty to thirty minutes.

Tortillas

Packages of the finished product are available in most markets in the western United States and, of course, Mexico. But there is something very rewarding about making your own. We were parked in a true wagon train circle at the north rim of the Grand Canyon. The fire in the middle of the circle was huge and warm and friendly. As the different families began their evening meal, coals were raked to one side of the fire. Fresh-made tortillas were thrown right on the coals and quickly cooked. Hands were ready to receive the toasty goodies. Some were eaten with butter and salt and pepper, others were filled and rolled with chili and some were filled with cheese. I only hope the early pioneers fared as well.

The tortillas can be formed with the palms of your hands and are done so beautifully in Mexico. We have a tortilla press that we lovingly pack along, a luxury but one we throughly enjoy.

Method 1
(makes 1 dozen six inch tortillas)

2 cups Masa (corn flour)
1 cup water

Shape twelve balls and let rest ten minutes. Form into six inch flat thin circles with your hands or by using a tortilla press. If using a press be sure to put wax paper or plastic wrap on both surfaces to prevent sticking. Cook and serve the same as Method 2.

Method 2
(makes 8 six inch tortillas)

Most stores carry the bags of Masa Harina in various weights. Usually the stores will have both corn and flour. If, however, you do not find it in your area, this recipe will suffice.

1 cup cornmeal	**1 teaspoon salt**
½ cup flour	**½ cup water**

Add more or less water to make a very stiff dough that will stick together. Let rest thirty minutes. Shape into small balls and press into thin flat six inch diameter circles. Fry on both sides in a skillet with enough grease to prevent sticking. Turn once. Serve with butter and salt and pepper open or folded in half or rolled. Fill with cheese, chili, green chilies etc.

Yorkshire Pudding

Although this recipe gives one the feeling of elegance, it is simple to prepare and adapts to many fillings. The roast beef is, of course, first choice but any leftover meat blended with a cream sauce becomes a fancy main course.

2 eggs	½ teaspoon salt
1 cup milk	1 tablespoon hot beef drip-
1 cup flour	pings

Blend all ingredients together with a mixer or rotary beater. Beat from three to five minutes. Let stand thirty minutes and beat one full minute at cooking time. Use the roasting pan with about three tablespoons beef drippings left in it when serving with a roast. Have the drippings sizzling hot and pour in the batter. Bake in a 400° oven twenty to twenty-five minutes until puffy and browned.

When using a muffin tin for individual servings, put one-half teaspoon shortening in each muffin tin and heat before adding the batter two-thirds full. Bake fifteen to twenty minutes. Open top to add a creamy filling.

Breads that Travel

When staying in one location for a period of time, I like to bake bread. The aroma seems to hug us all amidst a warm family experience. If you don't want to take the time while traveling, make at home and take along. All the breads freeze well. Spread with cream cheese, soft butter or peanut butter. It makes a gourmet lunch.

Old-Fashioned Oatmeal Bread
(makes 2 loaves)

4 to 4½ cups flour	2 packages dry yeast
¼ cup sugar	1 cup milk
1½ teaspoons salt	½ cup water
1½ cups oatmeal	⅓ cup shortening
	2 eggs—slightly beaten

In a large bowl, combine 1½ cups of the flour, sugar, salt, oatmeal and yeast. Mix milk, water and shortening and heat in a saucepan until shortening is melted. Cool to room temperature and gradually add to dry ingredients. Beat two minutes at medium speed on mixer. Add eggs and one cup flour. Beat at high speed until blended. Using a wooden spoon, work in the rest of the flour until you have a stiff, nonsticky, batter. Cover and let rise until doubled in bulk. This usually takes forty minutes to one hour on a warm sunny day. Stir down and beat vigorously one-half minute. Turn into two greased loaf pans. Bake in a 375° oven forty-five to fifty minutes. Remove from pans, brush the tops with butter and cool on racks.

Pumpkin Bread
(makes 3 to 4 loaf pans)

One of the easiest of the breads. No need to knead and the mixing is done in a jiffy. Great for school lunches at home or picnics on the road.

4 cups flour	½ teaspoon cloves
2 teaspoons baking soda	1½ teaspoons salt
1 teaspoon baking powder	3 cups sugar
1 teaspoon nutmeg	1 cup cooking oil
1 teaspoon cinnamon	1 can pumpkin—16 oz. size
1 teaspoon all spice	⅔ cup cold water
	4 eggs

In a large bowl, sift the flour, soda, baking powder, nutmeg, cinnamon, allspice, cloves, salt and sugar together. Make a well in the center and pour in the cooking oil, pumpkin and water. Blend well. Add the eggs one at a time, beating after each addition. Pour batter into three or four well greased loaf pans two-thirds full. Bake in a 350° oven one hour. Cool on wire racks.

Next Halloween, spread thin slices with cream cheese or butter. Your trickers will get quite a treat.

Zucchini Bread
(makes 1 large loaf)

1½ cups grated raw zucchini	1½ cups flour
1½ cups sugar	1 teaspoon baking powder
2 eggs	½ teaspoon baking soda
¼ cup cooking oil	¾ teaspoon cinnamon
½ teaspoon vanilla	¼ teaspoon nutmeg
	¼ teaspoon salt

Once I doubled the recipe because I wanted to give one loaf to a friend. The doubled recipe makes three bread pans.

Grate the zucchini. Spread it out on a flat plate, then set another plate on top to force excess liquid out. Let stand for one hour, pouring off excess liquid as needed.

Mix the sugar, eggs, oil, and vanilla together. Combine flour, baking powder, soda, cinnamon, nutmeg, and salt. Add to the first mixture and blend well. Grease and lightly dust the baking pans with flour. Pour in the batter. Bake in a 350° oven for one hour. Test with a toothpick or broom straw. Make sure it comes out clean. If not, continue cooking until it does, testing every five minutes. If you do not cook it long enough, it will be soggy in the middle. The cooking time will vary because of the amount of water in the zucchini.

Baking Mix

There are several baking mixes available and they are easy to use. However, here is one you can mix up and take along. There is a little creative appeal here.

9 cups sifted flour   **1 tablespoon salt**
¼ cup baking powder   **2 cups vegetable shortening**

Mix flour, baking powder and salt together in a large bowl. Add the shortening and work with a pastry blender until well mixed. The mixture should contain no pieces of shortening larger than half a green pea. Store in tightly covered container in a cool place. Use as you would a commercial mix.

Biscuits
(makes 1 dozen)

You may pat the dough out flat with your hands or roll with a glass or plastic drinking tumbler in case you do not have a rolling pin. You can cut in squares or into rounds with the top of a can or glass if you have left the biscuit cutter at home.

2 cups mix
½ to ¾ cup milk

Add the milk until you have a dough you can handle. Too much milk will make a dough too sticky to handle and not enough will make a dry, tough dough. Turn with a spoon, and a ball should form. It is OK for the dough to be sticky. Turn out on a floured surface and knead enough to make the dough roll out without sticking to the rolling pin. Cut into rounds or squares. Bake on ungreased baking sheet or cake pan ten to twelve minutes.

Shortcake

For shortcake biscuits to serve with fruit, add one table-spoon shortening and cut into the mix before adding the milk.

Muffins

These really add to a breakfast or dinner. You can vary them by adding nuts, raisins, fruits, blueberries or cinnamon. Make up your own additions.

2 cups mix	1 cup milk
3 tablespoons sugar	2 tablespoons melted shorten-
1 egg—slightly beaten	ing

Stir the sugar into the mix. Add egg, milk and shortening. Stir until just blended. Do not beat. Spoon into greased muffin tins two-thirds full. Bake in a 400° oven fifteen to twenty minutes.

Variation: Bake in a cake pan and sprinkle top with:

> 2 tablespoons mix
> 2 tablespoons brown sugar
> 1 teaspoon cinnamon
> 2 tablespoons butter

Mix all ingredients together and sprinkle on top of batter. A nice coffee cake for breakfast is the result. You will need to bake it twenty-five to thirty minutes.

Aloha Muffins
(makes approximately 1 dozen)

2 cups mix	¼ cup coconut
2 tablespoons sugar	1 cup pineapple yogurt
½ teaspoon baking soda	2 tablespoons cooking oil
	1 egg

Combine mix, sugar, baking soda and coconut. Add remaining ingredients and stir until blended. The mixture will resemble a soft dough rather than a muffin batter. Fill greased muffin tins two-thirds full. Bake in a 400° oven for fifteen to eighteen minutes.

Makes a good dessert too.

Maple Muffins
(makes approximately 1 dozen)

1 egg	1 tablespoon baking powder
¼ cup milk	¼ teaspoon salt
1¾ cup flour	⅓ cup maple syrup
	¼ cup melted butter

Beat egg and milk together in a bowl. Sift the flour, baking powder and salt together and add to liquid mixture. Stir in the maple syrup a little at a time. Fold in the melted butter. Fill greased muffin tins two-thirds full. Bake in a 350° oven twenty to twenty-five minutes.

Maple Biscuits

1 dozen biscuits
½ teaspoon cinnamon
¾ cup maple syrup

Put biscuits into a greased baking pan with edges touching. Sprinkle the cinnamon evenly over the tops. Heat the maple syrup until bubbly. Pour over the biscuits. Bake in a 400° oven fifteen to twenty minutes. Serve with butter.

Variation: Serve as a dessert with whipped cream or ice cream.

Spoon Bread

Serve with stews, omelets and creamed meats. Also good with fried fish in place of potatoes or hush puppies.

2 cups milk
1½ cups cornmeal
3 eggs—separated

1 tablespoon melted butter
½ teaspoon baking powder
1 teaspoon salt

Heat milk to the boiling point. Stir in cornmeal and continue stirring until thickened. Remove from fire. Beat egg yolks until light and lemon colored. Blend into cornmeal mixture. Add melted butter, baking powder and salt and blend well. Beat egg whites until stiff but moist and fold into blended mixture. Pour into a buttered baking dish so that mixture is at least two inches deep. Bake in a 350° oven thirty to forty minutes until a knife comes out clean when inserted.

Bacon Skillet Bread
(serves 4 to 6)

A great breakfast with scrambled eggs.

½ lb. bacon
2 cups flour
2 tablespoons sugar

1 tablespoon baking powder
1 teaspoon salt
1½ cups milk

Fry bacon until nearly done. Remove from skillet and cut into small pieces. Drain all but about two tablespoons bacon drippings. Arrange bacon evenly over the bottom of the skillet. Mix dry ingredients together and add milk. Blend well and pour over bacon. Cover and cook over medium-low heat twelve to fifteen minutes. Turn with a spatula and cook ten to twelve minutes more. Cut in wedges to serve.

SAUCES AND MARINADES

Make these up at home or along the way. Use any sauce or marinade that you use at home just as it comes from the bottle or with other things added.

Brush on as you cook, marinate overnight, or soak several hours before cooking.

It is great to tenderize and add flavor at the same time with so little fuss and preparation.

Marinade for Beef

¾ cup soy sauce
½ cup red wine

1 clove garlic minced
1 teaspoon curry powder
¼ teaspoon ground ginger

Combine all ingredients and store in a jar until ready to use.

Marinade for Poultry

½ cup honey
½ cup orange juice

¼ teaspoon salt
¼ teaspoon Spike

Combine all ingredients and store in jar until ready to use.

Marinade for Fish

½ cup white wine
½ cup water
1 tablespoon lemon juice
2 sprigs parsley

1 bay leaf
1 medium slice onion
3 peppercorns
¼ teaspoon celery salt

Combine and simmer five minutes, cool and marinate fish.

Spicy Marinade

1 cup catsup
¼ cup wine—red or white

1 tablespoon lemon juice
1 teaspoon chili powder
1 teaspoon horseradish

Combine all ingredients and store in a jar until ready to use.

Barbecue Marinade

½ cup catsup
½ cup soy sauce
½ cup melted butter

¼ teaspoon onion salt
¼ teaspoon paprika
3 drops hot sauce—optional

Combine all ingredients and heat in a saucepan. When sauce is hot, dip meat pieces into hot sauce to coat evenly. Barbecue over open fire. Brush with extra marinade.

Basting Sauce

½ cup butter—melted
½ teaspoon chili powder

¼ teaspoon salt
¼ teaspoon monosodium
glutamate—optional

Mix ingredients and use to baste chicken, turkey or shrimp. Cook over a grill or bake in the oven, basting often.

It is said that centuries ago, sauces and marinades were

conceived as a way to mask the odor or fact that food was perhaps spoiled. Maybe it's true, but we feel that a more punctuating flavor to enhance various foods calls for these tasty amenities, at home or away.

Keen Kabobs

The simplest of all food fare. Easy to prepare and easy to serve. The combinations are endless. Repetition is not necessary unless you do so by choice or request.

Use metal or bamboo skewers. The bamboo skewers come in several different sizes. They eliminate cleanup since they are discarded after use.

Vegetable Kabobs

> green peppers
> cherry tomatoes
> small white onions

Cut green pepper into one and a half inch wedges. Alternate with cherry tomatoes and small onions. Cook over the grill, under the broiler, or in a skillet.

Stew on a Skewer

1 inch chunks beef, veal or
  lamb
small mushrooms—canned or
  fresh

small onions—canned or fresh
small potatoes—canned
1″ wedges green pepper
1 can baby carrots

Alternate pieces on a skewer. Brush with oil and garlic salt. Cook over a grill, under the broiler or in a skillet. Turn often.

Chicken Kabobs

1½ inch pieces chicken—white and dark meat	1 can pineapple chunks slices of bacon 1 can button mushrooms

Begin and end with chicken pieces. Alternate chicken, pineapple chunks, bacon and mushrooms. For ease in handling and cooking. cut the bacon strips in half. Fold each half slice over itself before skewering. By running the skewer through a double thickness of bacon, it will not break and ravel off the skewer.

Skewered Shrimp

3 to 4 medium shrimp per person	butter dill

Clean shrimp, shell and devein. Leave the tails on. Run the skewer through the tail, twist the shrimp and run the skewer through the front meaty part. Push the shrimp close together. Brush with butter and sprinkle with dill. Cook over a grill or under the broiler or in a hot skillet. Turn frequently.

Other Things to Skewer

leftover fish chunks	vegetables
leftover meat	scallops
beets	hot dogs
sausage	meat balls

On occasion, when the dessert larder is low or tastes require a drastic change, we skewer bits of fresh fruit such as bananas, peaches, apple, oranges and the like. Sprinkle granulated sugar on generously or dredge through honey. Grill over an open fire and develop an unusual dessert fare.

CANDIES

Candy bars are sort of standard equipment in most recreational vehicles. They serve many purposes. A substitute for dessert, in between snacks, before bedtime treats and a source of energy for the hikers and fishermen. Frozen in the freezer in the summer they make a cool treat. They are good cut up in chunks in ice cream. Try melting several and blending with whipped cream for an instant pie filling.

Parked alongside a clear lake listening to the night sounds making homemade candy is quite a combination. Some candies are too involved and better left for the home kitchen. Here are a few uncomplicated ones that travel well.

Gusto Fudge
(makes 1 standard cake pan)

⅔ cup water
2 squares chocolate (2 oz.)
2 cups sugar
¼ teaspoon salt

1 tablespoon light corn syrup
¼ cup butter
1 teaspoon vanilla
½ cup finely chopped
    nuts—optional

Put water and squares of chocolate in the bottom of a double boiler. Melt the chocolate over very low heat. When the chocolate is almost melted, add one cup of the sugar. Bring to a boil and add remaining cup of sugar. Stir to blend. Add salt and syrup. Let boil over medium heat, stirring occasionally until four drops of mixture run off the edge of the spoon and run into one thick stream. At this stage a drop or two immersed in cold water should form a soft ball. Remove from heat. Add butter and vanilla. Do not stir. Wait until the sides of the pan are barely warm. Add nuts and beat vigorously for forty-five seconds to one minute. Pour into a buttered cake pan. Let cool and cut into squares.

This fudge is unusual because it is made with water and not milk.

Popcorn Balls

Popcorn is a favorite snack and age doesn't enter into it. Hot buttered popcorn has an aroma all its own. For something special and a little out of the ordinary, try popcorn balls. They are fun to make and very satisfying.

3 quarts popped corn	⅓ cup water
1 cup sugar	¼ cup butter
⅓ cup light corn syrup	¾ teaspoon salt
	1 teaspoon vanilla

Keep popcorn warm while making syrup. Cook sugar, light corn syrup, water, butter and salt to the hard crack stage, 270° on a candy thermometer. Remove from heat and add vanilla. Drizzle over warm popcorn. Mix with hands and form into balls the size of a baseball. Press hands together while molding popcorn into balls. Set on wax paper or greased platter to cool.

At holiday time, tint the syrup red or green and form the balls. Wrap in plastic wrap to store.

Crazy Nut Crunch

If you like popcorn and you like candy, this is for you because that is exactly what it is: popcorn candy. We think this is a marvelous gift for any holiday or birthday. When traveling in caravan it is just the thing for an unexpected birthday celebration.

2 quarts popped corn	1⅓ cups sugar
¾ cup chopped pecans	1 cup butter
¾ cup chopped walnuts	½ cup light corn syrup
⅔ cup toasted almonds	1 teaspoon vanilla
	salt to taste

Mix popped corn and nuts together and spread evenly on a baking sheet (may take two). Combine sugar, butter and syrup in a saucepan. Bring to a boil, stirring constantly. Continue boiling, stirring occasionally for ten to fifteen minutes until light caramel in color. Remove from heat and add vanilla. Drizzle over popped corn and nuts as evenly as possible. Toss lightly until well mixed. Spread it out to dry. Break apart and store in tightly covered container.

Chinese New Year

We can't really trace the origin to China but a friend got this recipe from a friend who happened to be Chinese. The first time we had them it was also New Year's Eve, not Chinese New Year. But, that's the way the cookie crumbles . . . an old Chinese proverb?

1 package semi-sweet choco- late bits	5 oz. Chinese noodles
1 package caramel bits	1 can Spanish peanuts
	½ cup yellow seedless raisins

Melt chocolate and caramel bits over hot, not boiling water. Mix noodles, peanuts and raisins in a very large bowl. Pour the melted mixture over the top and mix well with a large wooden spoon. Drop by teaspoonfuls on waxed paper. Chill in the refrigerator to set, then store in the refrigerator or at room temperature. We like them both ways.

Peanut Butter and Date Balls

Our middle son made this candy in third grade and it has been one of his specialities ever since. Very tasty and very nutritious.

½ cup peanut butter
1 cup finely chopped dates
2 tablespoons lemon juice

¼ teaspoon salt
½ cup sifted confectioner's sugar
¼ teaspoon nutmeg

Mix peanut butter, dates, lemon juice and salt together. Roll in the palms of your hands to form three-fourth inch round balls. When all the dough has been formed coat with confectioner's sugar and nutmeg by putting the sugar and nutmeg in a paper sack. Drop the date balls in a few at a time. Shake the bag to coat evenly. Store in covered container.

These are good chilled or unchilled. For a little variety, roll the dough around a pecan, walnut or almond before coating.

Crispy Fudge Squares
(makes 2 to 3 dozen squares)

A cookie-like batter that cooks up crisp like a candy. Very different. If you like fudge brownies you will surely want to try these Crispy Fudge Squares. The amount the recipe will yield depends on the size squares they are cut into—a one inch square makes a little over three dozen. A one and a half inch square will make approximately two dozen.

1 rounded cup semi-sweet
   chocolate bits
½ cup butter
¾ cup brown sugar—packed

1 teaspoon vanilla
1½ cups flour
1 teaspoon baking powder
½ teaspoon salt
¾ cup chopped nuts

Melt chocolate bits over hot water. Cream butter and sugar and add vanilla. Sift flour, baking powder and salt together. Add to the creamed mixture. This will be a very dry flaky mixture. You may have to use your hands, but don't expect the dough to hold together. Add chocolate and nuts and blend well. Spread in an ungreased 9 x 13 inch baking pan. Pack down firmly with your hand. Bake in a 350° oven eighteen to twenty minutes. Cool slightly and cut in squares.

Butterscotch Chips

If this recipe doesn't freak you out, I don't know one that will. This one is really out of sight.

4 cups butterscotch bits
1 cup cashew nuts
1½ cups French fried potato straws

Melt the butterscotch bits over hot water. Chop the cashew nuts very coarse and mix with potato straws. Stir together and drop by spoonfuls on waxed paper to harden. Store in airtight container. Serve at room temperature or chilled in the refrigerator.

Peanut Brittle

Yes, real honest to goodness peanut brittle. The beautiful thing about the recipe is that it only takes about fifteen to twenty minutes from conception to eating.

   The only thing you need is a wooden spoon and the ability not to panic over the last step of preparation.

We have amazed friends at home and on the road with this authentic and easy candy.

1 cup sugar
¼ cup baking soda
½ cup Spanish peanuts

Everything is done quickly, quickly, quickly. Put the sugar in a frying pan (cast iron skillet if you have one). Over medium low heat, melt sugar. It will become a deep caramel color. Shake pan often so as not to burn the sugar. The minute the sugar is completely melted remove from heat and quickly stir in baking soda and Spanish peanuts simultaneously. With a rubber spatula blend and pour onto a greased baking sheet or platter, as fast as you can. It begins to set up immediately. Let cool. Break into pieces and enjoy.

Our first attempt at this was in a motor home on a back road in central Canada and it was pouring rain at dusk. It was so successful, we devoured it in minutes, washed the skillet and made another batch. We hope you'll develop fond memories with it too.

COOKIES

If one word were used to describe cookies on a trip, whether a year or a weekend, the word would be—a MUST. When you have an attack of the "munchies" there is nothing like a cookie to satisfy that craving. If you plan a two to three week trip, the cookies can be made at home and stored in tins to travel. If you are going to be gone for a long period of time, plan the easiest and quickest recipes for baking in the vehicle.

For children, there is something quite comforting about having the "family favorites" along. So try some of these recipes, but be sure to include your own too.

Cookies can be part of lunch, desserts, and midafternoon and late night snacks. It sounds ridiculous but I know of one family who fed their finicky three year old oatmeal cookies and milk for breakfast. When you come right down to it, it was a very nourishing breakfast. The child was happy and so were they.

When the crew is fishing all day, no one wants to stop for lunch. Pack up a bunch of cookies for each member of the group.

Do take some along—whatever kind you particularly like. They are good anytime you wish to serve them.

148

Double Chocolate Marshmallow Brownies
(makes 9 inch by 13 inch pan)

2 eggs
1 cup sugar
2 squares unsweetened melted
   chocolate
⅓ cup butter
1 teaspoon vanilla

⅔ cup flour—sifted
½ teaspoon baking powder
¼ teaspoon salt
¾ cup minature marshmallows
½ cup semi-sweet chocolate
   bits

Beat eggs and sugar until light and fluffy. Melt the chocolate and butter together, add vanilla and blend into creamy mixture. Sift flour, baking powder and salt together and add to chocolate mixture. Stir in marshmallows and chocolate bits. Spread in a buttered 9 x 13 x 2 inch pan. Bake in a 350° oven twenty to thirty minutes. Cool and cut into squares.

Lemon Bars
(makes 8 inch square pan)

This is a recipe for lemon lovers. Most lemon cookies are flavored with a mild lemon. These are lemony lemon and very tangy. The smaller you cut the squares the farther they will go. They are so rich and delicious they are in regular demand on most outings.

½ cup soft butter
1 cup flour
¼ cup confectioner's sugar
2 tablespoons lemon juice

½ teaspoon grated lemon rind
2 beaten eggs—slightly beaten
1 cup sugar
2 tablespoons flour
½ teaspoon baking powder

Mix together soft butter, flour and confectioner's sugar. Pack this mixture into the bottom of an 8 inch square cake pan. Bake for fifteen minutes at 350°. Remove from oven and cool slightly. Mix lemon juice, grated lemon rind, eggs, sugar, two tablespoons flour and baking powder together.

Spread on the baked bottom crust. Bake twenty to twenty-five minutes in 350° oven. Cool twenty minutes and frost with the following glaze type icing.

¼ cup lemon juice
2 tablespoons water
confectioner's sugar—sifted

Mix lemon juice and water together. Add the sifted confectioner's sugar until the consistency is fairly thick but runs easily off a spoon. Pour and spread over baked mixture. When thoroughly cooled cut into squares. Store in airtight container in refrigerator.

No Bake Cookies

Ready to eat in a jiffy. Children love to help stir them. Serve chilled or room temperature. If you need dessert and haven't planned one, don't tell a soul, just say, "Tonight's project is dessert. Who wants to help?"

⅓ cup cocoa
½ cup milk
½ cup butter or margarine

2 cups sugar
3 cups oatmeal
⅓ cup crunchy peanut butter
1 teaspoon vanilla

Put cocoa, milk, butter, sugar, and oatmeal in a saucepan. Bring to a boil. The minute the mixture starts to bubble, boil exactly *one minute*. Stir constantly to prevent sticking. Remove from heat and add peanut butter and vanilla. Mix well. Drop by spoonfuls on waxed paper to cool. When they are hardened, remove to a plate or cookie tin. This is a great recipe for those in a vehicle without an oven. Range top cookies are quite an innovation.

Variation: Add chopped walnuts, pecans or peanuts to the cooked mixture.

Cake Mix Cookies

We've made these cookies from just about every kind of cake mix available. Spice, white, yellow and chocolate. For the first one, you might like to begin with a white or yellow. The variations are limitless so use your imagination.

> 1 box cake mix
> ¼ cup shortening
> ¼ to ⅓ cup milk

Place cake mix in a bowl. Cut in the shortening with a knife or pastry blender. Add milk to make a rollable dough for cutout cookies or until dough forms a ball for drop cookies. Bake in a 400° oven for eight to ten minutes.

Variations: Add one of the following:

> 1 teaspoon grated lemon rind
> 1 cup coconut
> 1 cup raisins
> ⅓ cup peanut butter
> ½ cup chopped nuts
> whatever else your little heart desires

Luscious Bars
(makes approximately 16 squares)

Our daughter absolutely adores these. They are a bit on the expensive side but so rich and mouth-watering, you'll want to include them somewhere on your trip. They are very satisfying so one is usually plenty. They are relatively easy to prepare and the ingredients are easy to transport.

½ cup butter	1 cup semi-sweet chocolate bits
1 cup graham cracker crumbs	1 cup chopped nuts
1 cup flaked coconut	1 can (15 oz.) condensed milk

151

Melt butter in a 9 x 9 x 2 inch pan. Sprinkle in layers in the order given. Pour the condensed milk over all. Bake in a 350° oven for 30 minutes. Cool in pan. Cut in squares when cooled. Serve at room temperature or chill in the refrigerator.

Carrot Cookies

Or what to do with last night's cooked carrots. Of course, if you are smart you will plan to have exactly one cup of leftover cooked carrots from the dinner menu. These cookies are both wholesome and delicious. A great way to serve vegetables to those in your family who proclaim they do not care for carrots.

¾ cup sugar
¾ cup shortening
1 egg
1 cup mashed cooked carrots
1 teaspoon vanilla

2 cups flour—sifted
2 teaspoons baking powder
¼ teaspoon salt
1 small handful of raisins—
    optional

Cream shortening and sugar until well blended. Add egg, mashed carrots and vanilla. Sift flour, baking powder and salt together and add to carrot mixture. Fold in raisins. Drop by spoonfuls on a greased baking sheet. Bake in a 350° oven twelve to fifteen minutes.

Variation: For extra fancy cookies, frost with white icing. Blend confectioner's sugar with just enough milk to make of spreadable consistency.

Butterscotch Crispies

1 cup sugar
1 cup light corn syrup
1 cup peanut butter
6 cups Rice Krispies cereal

1 6 oz. package semi-sweet
    chocolate bits
1 6 oz. package butterscotch
    bits

Bring sugar and corn syrup to a boil in a rather large saucepan. Remove from heat. Blend in the peanut butter and Rice Krispies. Press into a well-buttered 9 x 13 x 2 inch pan. When cooled ice with chocolate and caramel bits that have been melted together over hot (not boiling) water. Chill until set. Cut in squares.

Cooked Cereal Cookies
(makes about 4 dozen)

Next time you have leftover cooked hot cereal at the break-fast table, don't despair, make a batch of nourishing cookies.

⅓ cup shortening	½ teaspoon salt
1 cup brown sugar	1 teaspoon cinnamon
1 egg	¼ teaspoon nutmeg
1 cup cold cooked cereal	¼ teaspoon ginger
1¼ cup flour	1 cup seedless raisins
½ teaspoon baking soda	½ cup chopped nuts

Cream shortening and sugar together. Add egg and cereal. Sift flour, baking soda, salt, cinnamon, nutmeg and ginger together. Add to cereal mixture. Fold in the raisins and nuts. Drop by spoonfuls on a lightly greased cookie sheet. Bake in a 400° oven twelve to fifteen minutes.

Ice Box Cookies

These cookies will keep well in the refrigerator for several weeks. You may bake them fresh whenever you need them. We keep them in the freezer at home for several months. If your camper or motor home has a freezer, and many of them now do, keep them in the freezer and they will last indefinitely.

1 cup butter
1 cup brown sugar
1 cup white sugar
2 eggs—unbeaten
3 cups flour
1 teaspoon baking soda

1 teaspoon baking powder
1 teaspoon cinnamon
1 teaspoon vanilla
1 cup nuts—finely chopped
½ cup chocolate or but-
   terscotch bits

Cream butter and sugars together. Add eggs and blend well. Sift flour, baking soda, baking powder, cinnamon together. Add to creamed mixture. Add vanilla, nuts and butterscotch bits. Mix well and roll in waxed paper into two inch diameter rolls approximately twelve inches long. Chill overnight in the refrigerator or freeze until needed. Slice the roll into rounds about one-fourth inch thick and lay on a lightly greased cookie sheet about two inches apart. Bake in a 350° oven eight to ten minutes.

Variation: Spread with a thin layer of jelly or jam.

Chocolate Crinkles
(makes about 6 dozen)

These cookies have a rough textured surface which we find very interesting. We usually have a large supply on hand when traveling.

½ cup shortening
½ cup cocoa
2 cups sugar
4 eggs

2 teaspoons vanilla
2 cups flour
2 teaspoons baking powder
½ teaspoon salt
1 cup confectioner's sugar

Mix shortening, cocoa and sugar together. Blend in one egg at a time. Add vanilla. Mix flour, baking powder and salt together and add to chocolate mixture. Chill several hours or overnight. When ready to bake, preheat oven to 350°. Drop dough by teaspoonfuls, into the confectioner's sugar and roll around to coat evenly. Shape into a ball and place two inches apart on a greased baking sheet. Bake ten to twelve minutes. Do not overbake. They will come out of the oven fairly soft and will fall and crinkle.

Peanut Butter Cookies

I don't know which is more American, apple pie or peanut butter. I can't imagine a summer without either. If you want to turn these cookies into peanut butter and jelly, just spread jelly on a cookie and top with a second one.

1 cup brown sugar	2 eggs
1 cup white sugar	1½ cups flour
1 cup shortening	1 teaspoon soda
1 cup peanut butter—plain or crunchy	¼ teaspoon salt
	1 tablespoon vanilla

Cream sugars and shortening together. Add peanut butter and eggs. Blend well. Sift flour, soda and salt together and add to peanut butter mixture. Add vanilla. Make a ball about one inch in diameter, place about two inches apart on a greased baking sheet. With a dinner fork, press down on the top. Then turn the fork the opposite way and press again. The dough should be about one-fourth inch thick and look similar to a tic-tac-toe design. Bake in a 375° oven ten to twelve minutes until nicely browned. Store in an airtight container when cooled.

Old-Fashioned Oatmeal Cookies

Here is the family standby. The combination of good ole oatmeal cookies and a glass of cold milk is mighty hard to beat.

¾ cup shortening	½ teaspoon almond flavoring
1 cup brown sugar	1 cup sifted flour
½ cup white sugar	1 teaspoon salt
1 egg	½ teaspoon baking soda
¼ cup cold water	3 cups oatmeal (quick cooking)
1 teaspoon vanilla	1 cup raisins

Cream shortening and sugars. Add egg, water and flavorings. Sift flour, salt and baking soda together and blend into the creamed mixture. Add oatmeal and raisins. Blend well. The batter will be somewhat stiff so a wooden spoon is best. Drop by spoonfuls on a greased baking sheet. Bake in a 350° oven ten to twelve minutes until browned. They should be soft as they come from the oven. They will crisp as they cool.

For crisp cookies, store in an airtight container. For chewy cookies, store with an apple slice in the container.

Three for One Batter

These cookies keep well and freeze well. We have them in the freezer at home ready to put in our vehicle at a moment's notice. It is so helpful to make one cookie dough and have three different kinds of cookies from one baking.

This recipe makes an abundant number so you will need to plan an afternoon for baking. It yields approximately four dozen of each kind.

2 cups butter	2 teaspoons baking soda
3⅔ cups sugar	½ teaspoon salt
4 large eggs (or 5 small)	2 tablespoons vanilla
6⅓ cups flour	1 to 1½ cups semi-sweet choco-
4 teaspoons baking powder	late bits
1 teaspoon cream of tartar	1 to 1½ cups raisins

Cream butter and sugar. Add eggs one at a time and blend well after each addition. Sift flour, baking powder, cream of tartar, baking soda and salt together and add to creamed mixture. Add vanilla. Blend well. The dough should be a medium-soft consistency.

Divide the dough evenly into three separate bowls. Add chocolate bits to one, raisins to one and leave one plain. Drop by spoonfuls on a greased baking sheet. Flatten the plain ones slightly with the palm of your hand or the bottom of a glass. Bake in a 350° oven ten to twelve minutes.

Variations: Dust the plain cookies with granulated sugar. Add cinnamon or nutmeg to the sugar for some. Add figs, dates, nuts or any combination. Substitute butterscotch bits for the chocolate bits.

DESSERTS

Dessert is the last course of the meal. It can be as simple or elaborate as you wish. An elegant eight layered torte is impressive to serve but no more beautiful in the eyes of the beholder than a bowl of very fresh, deep red strawberries.

On the days when the scenery is breathtakingly beautiful, you will not want to spend time on the dessert course. There is nothing wrong with buying something to serve. Homemade ice cream and cookies may be wonderful at home but commercial ice cream and a packaged cookie may be just the thing while on vacation. Mother's Cookies in California packages a family size variety pack. There are speciality ice cream shops all over the United States, Canada and Mexico.

The following recipes will be easy to prepare or "do-ahead" and "take-along." How much you take will depend on the length of time you will be gone and the size of your vehicle.

Fruit and Cheese

Fresh fruit and cheeses are available almost everywhere. They make an elegant dessert wherever they are served, from fine restaurants to the most remote campsite. Try new exotic fruits and different flavors of cheeses that you might not experiment with at home. One family made a vacation project out of this dessert. Each member of the family chose a different fruit and cheese for each dessert on the trip. Lists were made of likes and dislikes and compared at the end of the vacation. The favorites were adopted for regular menus at home.

Dried Fruit Baked Pies

2 cups dried fruit	1 teaspoon grated lemon rind
2 cups water	1 teaspoon cinnamon
2 cups sugar	¼ teaspoon nutmeg
¼ teaspoon salt	2 tablespoons butter
juice of 1 lemon	pie crust recipe

Cook dried fruit with water until soft. Add sugar, salt, lemon juice and lemon rind. Simmer slowly until water is absorbed. Add cinnamon, nutmeg and butter and blend well. Roll out pie crust in six inch circles. Put filling on one-half of circle, generously but not out to edge. Fold other half over fruit and crimp edges together. Press edge of fork around edge to seal tightly. Bake in 425° oven about five minutes, then reduce heat to 325° and bake thirty to forty minutes longer until they are nicely browned. Leftovers keep well and are good hot or cold. They will warm up quickly.

Variation: Fry pies in about one inch hot oil for old-fashioned fried pies. Drain well before serving. Good as is or topped with ice cream.

Apple Pie

This filling is easily adaptable to a crust pie or bread pies cooked in a Toast Tight or Doughboy cooker. These can be purchased in sporting good stores or camper supply stores. They are round or square two-sided aluminum pans that open up. They have long handles so they can be used over the stove burners or over the campfire. The bread is buttered on one side, and placed buttered side down on each side of the Toast Tight. About two tablespoons of the filling is heaped in the middle of one side. When the handles are brought together and locked, the bread is crimped together with the filling in between. When cooked over heat, first on one side, then on the other, the finished product is a steaming apple pie. The handles open easily so you can peek inside to check the brownness.

To bake apple pie, the filling is heaped into a crust, topped with lattice or solid top crust and baked in a 425° oven for five minutes, then a 325° oven for thirty to forty minutes.

Apple Filling
(nine inch pie)

6 to 8 apples
½ to 2 cups sugar depending on tartness
juice of ½ lemon
1 teaspoon cinnamon
¼ teaspoon nutmeg
¼ teaspoon salt
¼ cup water
1 tablespoon flour
3 tablespoons butter

Peel and core apples, leaving enough peeling for color and flavor. Mix all ingredients together and simmer in a saucepan until apples are soft and tender. For the oven baked pie the mixture should be fairly liquid. For the Toast Tight pies, cook down until very thick.

Banana Flambé

1 banana for each person— unpeeled
foil to wrap bananas
1 teaspoon sugar for each banana
1 teaspoon high-proof rum or cognac for each banana

Wrap unpeeled bananas in foil. Put in the oven for twenty minutes. If you are using a campfire, lay on the coals for ten to twelve minutes. The banana will turn very dark, sometimes black over the coals, and become very soft. It will usually split open when ready. If it is very soft but has not split open, just slit one side with a sharp knife. Pour one teaspoon of sugar down the middle of each banana and mix slightly with a fork. Pour one teaspoon rum or cognac down the middle of each banana and ignite. It will flame beautifully and every one will be impressed, including you. We never cease to be amazed at how delightful this is to watch and so delicious to eat.

Variation: If children are along and do not like the taste of rum or cognac (the alcohol burns away), fill theirs with chocolate bits and marshmallows. Just split one side of the skin, mash the banana with a fork, add one or both and then wrap in foil. It will taste something like a very warm banana split.

S'Mores

For all the Girl Scouts in the world, this one will be a must. This is so good and so filling that we sometimes finish the dish washing and save these for later. They are especially good around a campfire. When we park where fires are allowed, it is most enjoyable to sit outside our home away from home, around a warm and glowing campfire. It's like having our own mountain cabin or beach cottage whenever we desire it. For each person you will need:

½ small Hershey bar (plain)	1 small piece of foil
2 graham cracker squares	napkin
	1 marshmallow

Lay the chocolate on one graham cracker square. Place on piece of foil and lay near the heat, if you like your chocolate melted. If you like your chocolate chewey, lay on a napkin away from the heat. Toast the marshmallow till brown and puffy. Place on the chocolate and top with second graham cracker. Press down and gently pull out stick or marshmallow toaster.

Butter Roll Pudding
(serves 6 to 8)

While in the midst of testing recipes, my husband decided to ask a business friend to join us for lunch. Lunch was ready when he arrived and we sat down to eat and converse. The topic of conversation was, of course, food. Our friend began to tell us of a boyhood aunt who used to make this delicious dessert from a biscuit recipe, butter, cinnamon and milk. He remembered watching her and the taste but nothing more. Intrigued, I began to make a batch of biscuits. I would ask him, "Is this what it looked like?" Sometimes I got a yes and sometimes a no. We all sampled the finished product and waited to see if it was exactly as he remembered. He thought and then tasted again. Then he nodded. The following recipe is an attempt to capture a boyhood memory and according to our friend is "mighty nearly perfect!"

2 cups flour
3 heaping teaspoons baking powder
1 teaspoon salt
¼ cup shortening

milk to make a dough you can handle
½ cup melted butter
1 tablespoon cinnamon
½ cup sugar
milk to cover top

Mix flour, baking powder and salt together in a bowl. Cut in shortening with a pastry blender or sharp knife. Add milk until the dough forms a ball and comes away from the sides of the bowl. It should be quite sticky at this point. Dump out on a floured board or cloth or wax paper, that has been generously sprinkled with flour. Knead a few times until it is no longer sticky. Roll out very thin. Brush with butter. Mix cinnamon and sugar together and dust all over evenly. Roll up jelly roll fashion. Cut in one inch pieces and place in a buttered baking dish so that the biscuits are touching on all sides. Then take your hand and press down on each biscuit making them fit very tight in the pan. Pour milk on the top to cover; approximately one-fourth inch thick. Bake in a 350° oven fifteen to twenty minutes until brown. They will be slightly damp in the middle but not soggy. This taste is so unusual, we hope you'll try it. Don't forget to bake longer if at a higher altitude.

Quick Cobbler
(serves 6 to 8)

Cobbler is a favorite of ours and we serve it often, on the go, at home for the family and at dinner parties. It is always well received.

½ cup butter (or 1 stick)
1 cup flour
1 cup sugar

1 teaspoon baking powder
¼ teaspoon salt
1 cup milk
1 cup fruit

Put butter in a 9 x 13 inch baking dish and place in a 325° oven. When butter is melted remove from oven. Mix flour, sugar, baking powder, salt and milk together and pour into the dish right on top of the melted butter. Put spoonfuls of fruit evenly on top of batter. Bake in 325° oven forty-five to fifty minutes.

You may use any canned or fresh fruit. If the fruit is fresh you may want to add sugar to taste. If you have one and one-half cups of fruit, go ahead and add it.

Variation: Use canned pie fillings.

Stacked Chocolate Creams
(serves 4)

1½ cups sour cream
1 cup semi-sweet chocolate bits
½ teaspoon cinnamon

20 cinnamon flavored graham crackers
¼ cup chopped nuts—
    peanuts, walnuts or almonds

Let sour cream stand at room temperature for fifteen minutes. If it's a very hot day, ten should be enough. Melt chocolate bits over low heat. Remove from heat and add cinnamon. Let cool five minutes, then blend with sour cream. Spread and stack five crackers for each serving making sure the filling in between oozes out sides. Then spread on top and smooth over the sides. Sprinkle nuts on top. Refrigerate all day or overnight.

Bread Pudding
(serves 6 to 8)

This delicious dessert can be made from fresh or stale bread. If there are children along, some of the stale bread will be saved for feeding the birds. I like to do this myself and have sometimes been called the "bird lady." It can be quite a fun project to put bread cubes in the branches of a small tree. Set a pan of water on the ground and you have an instant bird restaurant.

3 cups dry bread cubes	½ teaspoon salt
½ cup melted butter	3 eggs
1 cup dry milk	1 teaspoon vanilla
½ to ¾ cup sugar	1 quart hot water

If using fresh bread, let the bread stand at room temperature, uncovered for one hour. Lay the cubes evenly in the bottom of a 9 by 13 inch baking pan. Drizzle the melted butter over the cubes. Mix dry milk, sugar and salt together. Beat eggs and vanilla till light and lemon-colored, then add hot water until well mixed. Blend with the dry mixture and pour over the bread cubes. Bake in a 325° oven forty to fifty minutes or until golden and set.

Variation: After drizzling the butter over the bread cubes add one or all of the following:

1 cup raisins	1 teaspoon cinnamon
1 cup nuts—chopped	½ teaspoon nutmeg
1 teaspoon orange peel	Omit vanilla and use
1 teaspoon lemon peel	lemon or rum

Indian Pudding
(serves 6 to 8)

One of our friends makes a trip to New Hampshire to see her family once a year. Recently, she rediscovered her love of Indian Pudding. Her descriptions were so mouth watering we set out to try this traditional New England dessert. You try it too, you'll like it!

2½ cups milk
⅓ cup yellow cornmeal
1 cup cold water
½ cup sugar
½ cup molasses or sorghum
¼ cup butter

¾ teaspoon cinnamon
¼ teaspoon salt
¼ teaspoon nutmeg
¼ teaspoon ginger
2 eggs, slightly beaten

In the top of a double boiler, heat the milk to the boiling point. Mix the cornmeal with cold water and add to the hot milk. Continue to stir and heat until thick, about ten to fifteen minutes. Remove from heat and add sugar, molasses and butter. Let cool to lukewarm. Add seasonings and eggs and blend well. Pour in a greased pan and bake in a 300° oven for one and a half to two hours or until set. A knife inserted should come out clean. If you do not have an oven you can steam in the top of a double boiler till set. Let stand thirty minutes before serving. Serve warm.

Variations: Serve with one of the following:

> half and half poured over the serving
> whipped cream on top
> ice cream on top or on the side
> Hard sauce flavored with rum

Night and Morning Crab Apples

Little green apples from the store will make this recipe, but if you are lucky, pick your own crab apples. Many times you can obtain permission to pick apples from a privately owned orchard. Be sure to check with the owner first. We parked one night in a most unusual but delightful spot. A family had turned their orchard into a fantastic camping site for motor vehicles. Each vehicle had a private lane down the row of apple trees and at the end parked the vehicle. There was one available parking space at the end of each row of trees. Everyone who spent the night with them was asked please not to touch the fruit as this was their livelihood. We gladly respected their request. The family told us that even very small children were good about not picking fruit when told the reason.

**1 to 2 dozen crab apples—
the smaller they are the more
 you need
½ cup butter**

**juice of 1 lemon
1 to 2 cups sugar depending on
 tartness of fruit
½ teaspoon salt**

Wash and core enough crab apples to make a full quart. Peel leaving about one-fourth of the skin intact on each crab apple for flavor and color.

In a deep pan or a cast iron skillet, cook all ingredients together, stirring to prevent scorching. If you're out in cold weather, do this over an open fire. It's a great way to stay warm. Inside the vehicle on a rainy night, the delicious aroma of these buttery apples is unforgettable. If you have an oven, put the apple mixture in a pan after five minutes of cooking and bake slowly about forty-five minutes. If you do not have an oven, lower the heat after ten minutes of cooking and stir off and on for forty-five minutes, or until very thick. They are good served hot or cold, with the meal or as a dessert with whipped cream or ice cream or plain.

Save one cup of the mixture, cool and mash to a thick sauce. Add one teaspoon cinnamon and spread on the breakfast toast. Good eatin'!

Blackberry Cobbler

Blackberry vines are prevalent throughout Washington, Oregon and Canada. Many Southern states have an abundance of blackberry vines. In twenty minutes you can pick enough blackberries for a scrumptuous cobbler. Be sure to warn children and "first-timers" about the thorns (and, if in the South . . . about the "chiggers").

4 cups blackberries	1 tablespoon lemon juice
2 cups sugar	½ teaspoon salt
¼ cup butter	1 teaspoon cinnamon
2 tablespoons flour	¼ teaspoon nutmeg
	1 recipe pie crust

Mix all ingredients together and put into pie crust in a cast iron skillet or deep heavy pot. Cover with a top crust and seal the edges. Prick several holes in the top crust with the tines of a fork. Bake 325° for one hour.

Variation: If you do not have an oven this is a good alternative. This stove top variation is equally as good as the oven baked pie:

Cook blackberries in a pan on top of the stove or open fire about one hour. You will need to simmer very slowly and frequent stirring is necessary to prevent sticking and scorching. You'll find a young child delighted to remind you to stir. Make a biscuit batter and drop by spoonfuls onto a hot surface . . . like pan biscuits. When done, split open and put on a plate. Spoon blackberry mixture over the top like strawberry shortcake.

Helpful hint: If you have blackberry stains on your fingers, rub with lemon juice to remove.

Fast Doughnuts

There is no end to the many ways you can prepare refrigerator biscuits. This is another in the tasty variations.

Poke a hole, with forefinger or thumb, in the center of the

uncooked biscuit. Fry in one inch hot oil in a skillet, turning once. Drain on paper towel. When all have been cooked and cooled shake in a paper bag with granulated sugar or confectioner's sugar. Add cinnamon to the sugar for half if you wish.

Overnight Doughnuts
(makes 2 to 2½ dozen)

1 egg	3 tablespoons butter—melted
1 egg yolk	¼ teaspoon cinnamon
½ cup sugar	2 cups flour
½ cup milk	3 teaspoons baking powder
	oil for frying

Beat the egg and egg yolk until light and lemon colored. Slowly add the sugar, milk, butter and cinnamon. Blend well. Sift the flour and baking powder together four times and add to batter mixture. Chill overnight. Pinch off enough to make a small ball and poke your finger through the center to make a hole. Fry in deep hot oil. Eat plain or coat with sugar.

This dough will keep well in the refrigerator for several days. Store extra cooked doughnuts in a plastic bag or air-tight container.

Take Along Meringues

These meringues will keep for two to three weeks in an airtight container. Make them up before you leave and serve with ice cream, whipped cream, fresh fruit or pudding and pie filling. They make an elegant dessert with no fuss at all.

8 egg whites	¼ teaspoon cream of tartar
2¾ cups sugar	heavy brown paper—grocery
¼ teaspoon salt	bag will do

Whip egg whites until stiff but moist. Gradually add salt and two and one-fourth cups of the sugar that has been sifted twice. Fold in the other one-half cup sugar. Lay heavy brown paper on cookie sheets and drop mounds of the egg white mixture about four inches apart. With the back of a serving spoon, push an indentation in the center of each mound. Bake in a 250° oven thirty to forty minutes until meringues are very dry. Turn off oven, open door a crack and leave another twenty minutes. Remove from oven and cool. Remove from brown paper with a spatula. Store in airtight container.

Iced Angel Cake

1 loaf angel cake or small tube cake	**½ to 1 cup strawberries or raspberries**
½ pint heavy cream	**¼ to ½ cup sugar**

These small angel food cakes are available throughout the country in grocery stores of every size from small town markets to gigantic super markets. They will keep for several days. When ready to use, make at least two hours before serving. I have, on occasion, made them at the last minute but I feel that the flavor is a bit improved when made ahead. Slice the cake in thirds horizonally. Whip the cream and fold in the berries and sugar to taste. Ice the cake between layers and on top. It looks as good as it tastes.

Cool Banana Pie
(nine inch pie)

When we first started camping in the Sierras we did not have a motor home and we did not have a refrigerator. The weather was cold toward late afternoon and during the night. We would whip up this pie as the weather turned cool in the afternoon, set it in the engine compartment of our station wagon and by dessert time the pie was chilled and set. Of course it is just as good made in our refrigerator but it doesn't make as interesting a story.

1 recipe graham cracker pie crust (recipe follows)

2 bananas

1 package instant banana pudding mix

1 8 oz. package cream cheese

Prepare crust and press into a nine inch pie pan. Save one tablespoon of the crumbs to sprinkle over the top of the pie for decoration. Slice the bananas into the crust making an even layer. Prepare pudding according to packaged directions. Fold in the cream cheese which has been softened to room temperature. Pour over the bananas spreading smooth on top. Sprinkle with crumbs. Chill in the refrigerator until set and cool, one hour or overnight.

Variation: Sprinkle chopped salted peanuts on top.

Graham Cracker Pie Crust

The following recipe is for a nine or ten inch pie. When traveling, it is nice to have several recipes prepared ahead of time and individually packaged. When preparing ahead of time, mix all the dry ingredients together and package. When ready to make a pie, just add the butter and press into pie pan.

16 graham crackers

¼ cup sugar

½ teaspoon cinnamon

⅛ teaspoon salt

¼ cup melted butter

Mix dry ingredients together. Blend in butter until well mixed. Pat firmly in a pie pan. Bake five minutes in a 300° oven to set before filling.

Fluffy Tapioca Pudding
(serves 4)

Although this recipe will serve four people, our younger son has been known to devour the whole recipe in a single sitting. This is one of those easy recipes so easily overlooked.

3 tablespoons minute tapioca

5 tablespoons sugar

⅛ teaspoon salt

1 egg—separated

2 cups milk

1 teaspoon vanilla

Mix tapioca, three tablespoons sugar, salt, egg yolk and milk in a saucepan. Cook over medium heat, stirring constantly, until it begins to boil. Cook six to seven minutes until thickened. Remove from heat. Beat egg white until stiff but moist. Gradually beat in the other two tablespoons of sugar. Blend the hot mixture into the beaten egg white and blend well. Add vanilla. Serve warm or well chilled.

Pineapple Upsidedown Cake
(makes ten inch cast iron skillet)

Serve warm with fresh dairy whipped cream. If you are really lucky, buy some from a farm near by.

¼ cup butter	1 small yellow cake mix—
½ cup brown sugar	makes one layer
1 4 oz. can crushed pineapple	whipped cream

Melt butter in the bottom of cast iron skillet. Remove from heat and pat brown sugar evenly on top. Pour in crushed pineapple. Prepare yellow cake mix according to package directions and pour on top of pineapple. Bake in 325° oven twenty-five to thirty minutes until cake is done. Let cool in pan five minutes then turn out upsidedown on a platter. Use a spatula to gently lift underneath edges.

Rice Pudding

Old-fashioned rice pudding is quickly made with planned leftover rice. When preparing rice for a meal, make an extra 2 cups. Three-fourths of a cup uncooked rice will usually yield about two cups when cooked.

2 cups cooked rice	1 tablespoon melted butter
1⅓ cups milk	2 eggs
¼ cup sugar	1 teaspoon vanilla
¼ teaspoon salt	½ cup raisins

Combine all ingredients. Place in a greased baking dish and bake in a 325° oven twenty to thirty minutes or until set. Serve warm or cold, plain or with cream.

Maple Apples
(serves 4)

4 medium apples—peeled and cored

¼ cup water
¼ cup maple syrup
½ cup heavy cream

Place apples in a cake pan or heavy cast iron skillet.

Pour water and maple syrup over the apples. Bake in 325° oven forty-five minutes to one hour, basting often. If you want to cook on top of the stove, baste more frequently and cover for ten minutes at the end of cooking time if they are not tender. Serve warm or chilled with cream poured over them or topped with cream whipped thick, but not stiff.

Variations: Try maple syrup over pumpkin or peaches. Delicious canned or fresh. Sprinkle a little nutmeg over the cream for a still different taste treat.

Snow Cones

If you are in high country, there should be snow somewhere along the way. If not, try an ice house in town. Crushed ice is a good substitute but snow cone ice is better. It is very finely shaved and holds the flavor of the syrup longer.

For each person you will need a paper cup or cone filled with snow or shaved ice. Pour any concentrated punch syrup over the snow until the color is absorbed. Use a straw and keep sipping and stirring.

Some specialty stores have small, metal scrapers suitable for scraping snow from a block of ice.

Variation: When I was a child we loved going sledding in the snow, half for the fun of sledding downhill and half for the snow ice cream we enjoyed warming up afterwards.

1 cup snow for each person   1 tablespoon sugar
¼ cup milk or light cream   ½ teaspoon vanilla

Pack the snow tightly in a cup. Mix the milk, sugar and
vanilla together and pour over the snow. Stir to blend. Eat
with a spoon and go to the bottom of the cup for every bite.

Apricot Sherry Layer Cake
(one-pound pound cake)

Buy a one-pound pound cake and slice it into thirds hori-
zontally. Spread the layers with apricot jam and pour several tablespoons sherry over each layer of jam. Spread a
layer of whipped cream on each layer and stack back together. Ice the outside with whipped cream if desired and
chill before serving.

Sweet and Sour Fruit

This dessert is one of the most delightful served in one of
Los Angeles' finest restaurants. Trader Vic's serves strawberries, and although we adore them, we have also enjoyed
grapes, blueberries and boysenberries. You will need the
following:

1 bowl of fresh strawberries   1 bowl of brown sugar
1 bowl of sour cream   1 small serving plate for each
                                      person

Spear a strawberry. Dip and roll in the sour cream, then
dip and roll in the brown sugar. A savory morsel indeed.

Ambrosia

This is a favorite dessert in the South. It is light and cool
and makes a nice finish for a heavy meal. It is easy to
prepare and serve. The following will serve four persons.

3 bananas—sliced   ½ cup flaked coconut
3 large oranges—sectioned   2 tablespoons orange liqueur

I like to chill my fruit in the refrigerator one hour before serving but it certainly isn't necessary. Mix all together and serve.

Cherries Jubilee
(serves 4 to 6)

1 jar currant jelly   ¼ cup brandy
1 #2 can dark cherries   1 pint vanilla ice cream

Mix the jelly and cherries together in a saucepan. Heat until it begins to bubble. Remove from fire and add the brandy. Ignite and pour over the ice cream while flaming.

Brandied Mincemeat

Here is another great "over ice cream" dessert. This one is also served at our house during the Christmas holidays.

1½ cups boiling water   2 tablespoons cold water
1 cup sugar   ¾ cup prepared mincemeat
¼ cup butter   ½ cup brandy
1 tablespoon cornstarch   1 pint vanilla ice cream

Mix together the boiling water, sugar and butter. Mix the cornstarch and cold water together and add to the hot mixture.Blend in the mincemeat. When ready to serve, heat thoroughly and add the brandy. Pour over the ice cream. Flame if desired.

Cakes and Sauces

Cakes and sauces are easier to prepare, serve and store than iced cakes. You may use purchased cakes, any kind you prefer, or whip up the following recipe for pudding cake. It was originally baked in a wood stove in a cast iron skillet. I still use a cast iron skillet in a regular oven and the result is a smooth light brown coating when turned out on a plate.

The sauces are good prepared on the spot or made ahead and brought along in jars.

Pudding Cake

1 cup sugar
1 scant cup butter—or half
   margarine, half shortening
2 eggs
enough milk to fill cup—
   explanation follows

2 cups flour
2 teaspoons baking powder
¼ teaspoon salt
1 teaspoon vanilla

Cream butter and sugar together until smooth. Break the eggs in a cup and fill the cup with milk. The amount of milk is determined by the size of the eggs. Add to the creamed butter and sugar. Sift flour, baking powder and salt together and add to the liquid mixture. Add vanilla and beat until well blended. Pour into a greased cast iron skillet (ten to twelve inch) and bake in a 350° oven thirty to forty minutes until cake springs back when touched or a toothpick comes out clean when inserted. Let cool five minutes. Run a spatula around the edges and turn out on a platter. Serve with one of the following sauces.

Pudding Cake Sauce

Be sure to prepare this sauce before washing the cake bowl because it is started in the same bowl as the cake batter.

½ cup sugar
1 tablespoon cornstarch
¼ teaspoon salt

1 cup boiling water
2 tablespoons butter
½ teaspoon vanilla
½ teaspoon lemon flavoring

Blend sugar, cornstarch and salt together and add to the cake batter left on the sides and bottom of the bowl the cake was prepared in. Pour in the boiling water and add the butter and flavorings. Blend well. If it does not thicken sufficiently, cook several minutes on top of the stove, remembering that it will thicken more as it cools. Spoon over the pudding cake.

Variation: Add ice cream or whipped cream to each serving.

Chocolate Syrup
(makes 2 cups)

1 cup cocoa	¼ teaspoon salt
1 cup sugar	1 cup cold water
¾ cup light corn syrup	2 teaspoons vanilla

Mix all ingredients except vanilla in a saucepan. Place over low heat and stir until smooth. Raise heat and boil for three minutes, constantly stirring to prevent sticking and scorching. Add vanilla. Pour at once in jar or jars. Store in the refrigerator.

Caramel Sauce
(makes 2 to 2½ cups)

This sauce takes a bit of time and effort but the results are so mouth watering that it is well worth it. When served warm over vanilla ice cream and cake it makes caramel ice cream cake and when topped with whipped cream and a cherry, it becomes a dessert fit for a king.

2½ cups sugar	1 tablespoon cornstarch
1 cup milk	2 tablespoons butter
	1 teaspoon vanilla

Brown one cup of the sugar in a cast iron skillet. Watch it carefully so that it does not even begin to scorch. Shaking the skillet a bit will help prevent this. Stir with a wooden spatula when needed. Heat the remaining one and a half cups of sugar, milk, cornstarch and butter in a saucepan until it begins to bubble. Pour into the browned sugar and stir until smooth and thickened. Don't worry if it lumps up, it will stir down nice and creamy. Add vanilla and store in jars.

If not using right away store in the refrigerator. Let stand at room temperature one hour before serving as it tends to be quite thick when cold. It is marvelous when served warm.

Sour Cream Orange Sauce
(makes 2 cups)

¼ cup butter
1 cup confectioner's sugar
⅔ cup sour cream

⅓ cup fresh or frozen orange juice
1 teaspoon grated orange rind

Cream butter and sugar together until creamy. Beat in the sour cream, orange juice and grated orange rind. Store in jars in the refrigerator.

Variation: When serving, add fresh orange slices on top of the cake. Top with sauce and whipped cream flavored with one-fourth teaspoon nutmeg or cinnamon.

Something for the Kids
(makes 1 to 1½ dozen)

Buy several kinds of packaged or canned, ready-to-use icings before leaving home. Take along a large carton of ice cream cones, the flat bottom type. What you don't need for the cone cakes you will have on hand for ice cream cones—another no dish washing idea.

2 cups flour
1 cup sugar
1 tablespoon baking powder
½ teaspoon salt

¼ cup shortening—melted
1 cup milk
1 egg
1 teaspoon vanilla

Sift the dry ingredients together. Add the melted shortening to the milk, egg and flavoring mixed together. Combine the mixture and blend well. Pour into the cones two-thirds full. Stand in muffin tins or touching on a cookie sheet. Bake 350° oven for twenty minutes until golden brown. Cool and ice or better still, let the kids ice. They look like ice cream cones but taste like cake and icing.

Pineapple-Macaroon Pudding

1 package macaroon cookies
2 tablespoons butter
1 can crushed pineapple—
    drained

¼ cup honey
⅛ teaspoon almond flavoring
pinch of salt

Generously butter a Pyrex baking dish. Line with macaroon cookies. Reserve one-fourth of cookies. Mix pineapple, honey, almond flavoring and salt. Put mixture over cookies in baking dish. Crumble remaining macaroons over top. Bake in 300° oven for thirty minutes or until top is well-browned.

Remove from oven and rest for five minutes. Top with whipped cream or vanilla ice cream and a dash of nutmeg.

WINES

If you use and enjoy wines at home by all means take them along in your camper too. There are a great many occasions along your itinerary when wine can contribute to the overall enjoyment of any meal, especially if you're making a special event out of a nice catch of trout or any other more elaborate meal.

Selecting wines for travel can be a lot of fun before the trip and surely add pleasure to any meal along the way.

The fact that most wines are "cellared" indicates that they should be prepared for travel by packing the bottles on their sides, wrapped in paper and stored in the coolest part of the camper. Planning what to take and in what quantity should be thought out in advance. Take the best travelers. Both Pinot Chardonnay (a crisp white wine of good character) and Pinot Noir (a full-bodied red wine for most red meats) are excellent travelers. Obviously your favorites should be included.

White wines can be effectively chilled in a nearby stream. About two or three hours should be enough chilling time.

Allow more time if the river or creek is below three thousand feet altitude. We often set a bottle of red wine in the stream's edge for an hour or so before serving time, especially if the weather is very warm.

You won't want to take along your favorite crystal stemware for serving wines on the camper excursion but, on the otherhand, paper cups just don't make it either. We compromise. During the year. we save various, small glasses (the ones that contain cheese spread and the like). These are not very sophisticated but since wine served in glassware is enhanced in flavor the effect is much the same as when served in crystal.

If you insist on a more refined service technique, buy the throw-away plastic stemware. They look the part, even if the taste from the edge of a plastic rim doesn't match the pleasure of sipping wine from glassware.

Remember that good wines don't keep very well after opening because fermentation usually develops and the flavor is lost. So only take the size bottles which will be used at one meal. If you're going to take along gallon jugs of inexpensive "fortified" wines, be prepared for disappointment.

Dante Bagnani, our vice-president friend at California's Geyser Peak Winery, says, "Most California wines bottled today are good travelers." We find this to be true and use California natural wines almost exclusively.

In any event, a pleasant glass of good wine can even enhance the dining experience of a peanut butter sandwich and potato chips.

A Precaution Concerning Alcoholic Beverages in Your Camper

Since we do enjoy having wine along the way we feel that this precaution should be included.

Some years ago on an extended trip through Canada's west coastal area, knowing we would be away for five weeks, we carefully selected about two dozen bottles of our favored wines. When we crossed the United States border into Canada we were asked if we had alcoholic beverages. By answering truthfully, our wine (except the allowable volume of one-fifth) was confiscated and destroyed. There is no need to describe our disappointment (even anger) but after all, each country has the right to set its own importation laws and had we known in advance we would have been spared this trauma.

Sangria on the Go

The Spanish did a great deal more for us than to send Columbus out in his three little ships to discover the New World. They also produced a delightful concoction of table wine and various fruits and their juices called Sangria. There are numerous ways of producing this refreshing beverage and we have it often when traveling in our camper.

White Sangria

1 lemon, sliced
1 orange, sliced
1 cup strawberries, cut in
    fourths or sliced fresh
    peaches

¼ cup sugar
½ cup brandy—optional
2 fifths white chablis or other
    white table wine
12 ozs. club soda or lemon/lime
    soda or ginger ale

Put all ingredients into a large pitcher or Thermos jug after mashing the citrus a bit to render the juice. Chill and serve.

Variations: Pink Chablis or Vin Rosé are equally as good.

Depending on the season, we often find roadside stands at small farms and ranches selling fruits produced there. Usually the prices are very reasonable and the fruit uniquely fresh and vine-ripened. On various occasions we have used virtually every fresh fruit available in this recipe including Bing cherries, apples, pears, tangerines, apricots, berries, grapefruit and even watermelon. All seem to unite with the wine in a perfect marriage of refreshing flavors.

Tip: If the Sangria is finished the same day it's made we remove the various fruit bits and serve them as a small compote with a cookie for dessert.

OTHER BEVERAGES

Any trip into the out-of-doors requires more liquid in our diets. We are more active and we need more fluids to replace those lost through perspiration brought about by more physical exertion and exposure to the warmth of a summer day. What to drink and when to drink it should be considered in advance and although good, cool, potable water is generally available it is a good idea to think ahead sufficiently to make sure of having a proper supply wherever we are led to go on a camper excursion.

Many years ago it was possible to drink directly from a fast-moving mountain stream and enjoy the cold goodness of water which tumbles past thousands of square feet of rocks and sand from the melting snow and ice of the mountains above us. The water is the same but various pollutants are now present which were not there in years past.

Many millions now spend a great deal of leisure time in the outdoors. With those increased numbers have come ecological abuses such as using the stream nearby as a refuse dump. It is disturbing to see paper cartons, soft drink cans, plastic containers and raw garbage drifting along an otherwise magnificent stream. Many uninformed or careless campers even clean their fish at the water's edge, allowing the aftermath to float down the stream. These and other abuses make the act of drinking water from the average stream inadvisable if not totally foolish. For these and various other reasons, this once generous flow of cool and delicious drinking water is no longer suitable for human consumption. Plan ahead. If the camping area you select as a destination does not have drinking quality water, you'll need to bring your own.

Be prepared to instruct family members about this. Don't let them make the mistake of bending down to sip long draughts of the cool liquid from the campground stream in an imitation of John Wayne after a cattle drive across the Arizona wastelands. A good old-fashioned case of dysentary can ruin the entire trip for everyone, not just the one suffering from the malady.

If you have access to a small, portable water purifier, it can be a very handy thing to have along. Although these are generally capable of handling very small amounts of water for each filtering operation, they can come in handy when there is no assured source of pure drinking water.

If you suspect that there may not be potable water available at your destination, take along a number of plastic bleach jugs from your own laundry room. These may be rinsed out and used to take along a good supply, even if reserved only for emergency.

In addition, there are water purifying tablets with which to treat questionable water. Also, boiling water kills bacteria. In any case, the best rule of thumb is to exercise good sanitation practices away from home, for the same reasons as at home.

So much for drinking water. There are many other beverages which lend themselves to your camper. We make a practice of reducing the amount of commercial, canned or bottled soft drinks taken along. First, they are heavy, a nuisance to chill. and awkward to dispose of properly at times. Second, they don't seem to satisfy our thirst and aren't really that great for the system.

We have depended on a variety of other beverage forms

in the outdoors for so long, it is now a way of life. For example:

Good Choices on the Go

Thirst quenching liquids are a must. Everyone has a favorite. Ice water to me is the oasis on the desert. Other members of the family choose iced tea, lemonade and grape juice.

Sometimes the function of a beverage is to warm the soul. Hot tea, coffee and cocoa to name a few.

There is a certain beauty about a pitcher of ice cold lemonade in the shade of a tree on a summer's day and a mug of foamy hot chocolate around a campfire on a chilly night in the high mountains.

There are many commercial drinks on the grocery shelves. Canned, bottled and dry mixes are available everywhere. Stock your vehicle with your family favorites. Blend several different mixes for new treats.

Lime Lemonade
(serves 4 to 6)

If you prefer old-fashioned lemonade or old-fashioned limeade, just use all lemons or all limes (six of either). They say necessity is the mother of invention and that is exactly how this recipe was born. We were going to make a pitcher of limeade, when our son brought two new camp friend acquaintances to join us. Our cupboard had only three limes, so fortunately we added our only three lemons. Our friends were delighted with the refreshing new taste and took the recipe back to their trailer.

3 large limes
3 large lemons
¼ teaspoon grated lime rind

¼ teaspoon grated lemon rind
¾ cups sugar
1½ quarts water

Squeeze limes and lemons. Strain to remove seeds and pulp. Add rinds, sugar and water. Stir until well blended. Serve over ice cubes.

Instant Russian Tea
(makes 36 or more servings)

Mixture keeps indefinitely. Store in jars or one pound coffee cans. Be sure the lid is tight fitting. Great for individual servings and large punch bowls. For extra aroma, float slices of any citrus fruit in a cup or bowl.

14 ounces concentrated orange drink	¾ cup instant tea
6 ounces lemonade mix	½ cup brown sugar
	1 teaspoon cinnamon
	1 teaspoon ground cloves

Mix ingredients together until well blended. Store in airtight containers. Shake before using.

To Serve: 2 teaspoons per cup—for hot tea
3 teaspoons per mug—for hot tea
3 teaspoons per glass—for iced tea
½ cup per 1 quart serving

Just put mix in the bottom of glass or cup and fill with hot or cold water as needed.

For Those Who Think Young

Oddly enough our babies loved this and it is really a carry-over from their early days. We have found that many people either do not drink coffee or just don't like the taste. Try serving this instead and you may find yourself pleasantly surprised. Search until you decide upon your family's favorites.

any flavor Jello
¼ cup more water than package directions

Prepare Jello according to package directions. Let cool to room temperature and serve over ice.

Iced Coffee

Make extra coffee at mealtime. Store in the refrigerator until well chilled. Serve over ice plain or with cream and sugar. For a fancy treat add a scoop of vanilla ice cream. Serve with ice cream and a dash of Kahlua.

Vegetable Broth
(serves 4 to 6)

1 24 oz. can vegetable cocktail juice	2 teaspoons dried beef stock
	1 tablespoon lemon juice
	1 teaspoon chopped chives

Method for serving hot: Heat vegetable juice, beef stock and lemon juice until bubbly. Pour into mugs and sprinkle chives on top.

Method for serving cold: Heat one cup vegetable juice and add beef stock. Stir until dissolved. Add rest of the vegetable juice and lemon juice. Pour over ice and sprinkle with chives. You may chill in the refrigerator for several hours and omit serving ice cubes.

Cocoa Mix

Travel was the reason for this mix, but it was so satisfactory that it is now a staple item on our shelves at home. Prepare it right in an insulated paper cup and no cleanup is necessary.

2 cups unsweetened cocoa	8 cups dry non-fat milk
2 cups sugar	½ teaspoon salt

Mix thoroughly and store in airtight containers. Coffee cans are great. Even the can the cocoa came in stores a good supply.

To serve:

>   use ¼ to ⅓ cup for 1 cup boiling water
>   use ¾ cup for 1 pint boiling water
>   use 1½ cups for 1 quart boiling water

For added flavor, zest and fun add marshmallows or a dash of rum or stir with a cinnamon stick. For Mexican chocolate add one-fourth teaspoon ground cinnamon. Top with a dollop of sweetened whipped cream.

For a cold drink, use only enough boiling water to dissolve the mix. Fill glass with ice cold water and stir.

Beefy Bouillon

A great pick-me-up for between meals. Also a nice before dinner cocktail. Keeps well in the refrigerator and warms up in a jiffy. I personally also like it chilled.

2 beef bouillon cubes	2 teaspoons celery salt
4 cups boiling water	1 teaspoon onion salt
1 tablespoon lime juice	2 drops Tabasco sauce
1 tablespoon Worcestershire sauce	

Put bouillon cubes in a deep saucepan. Pour over them four cups boiling water. Add other ingredients and stir until completely dissolved. Serve in mugs or cups. Store in refrigerator.

Fruit Sodas

The fruit flavor of the soda will depend upon what fresh fruit is available in the area. We have used bananas, raspberries, peaches, strawberries, blackberries, and others.

>   2 scoops vanilla ice cream
>   ½ cup fresh fruit—peeled and mashed slightly
>   club soda to fill glass

Put one scoop of ice cream in the bottom of a glass. Wash and peel the fruit. Add to the glass and mash into the ice cream with a fork. The fruit should be somewhat broken up and blended slightly with the ice cream. Add club soda and stir. Top with second scoop of ice cream.

With cheese and crackers it makes a hearty luncheon fare.

Sherbet Cooler

Made with one kind of sherbet this cooler is delightful. Made with two compatible sherbets it is exotic.

2 scoops sherbet
club soda to fill glass
sprig of mint—optional

Put one scoop of sherbet in a glass. Fill two-thirds full with club soda. Stir till nearly blended. Add second scoop of sherbet and fill glass to rim with more club soda. Top with sprig of mint.

Hot Apple Cider

When traveling in the fall of the year, to sip hot apple cider out among the changing leaves is pure bliss. Once we were driving through northern California just before Thanksgiving. Two small boys had set up a roadside stand to sell pumpkins, sunflowers, Indian corn and decorative gourds. We stopped to buy several things for our Thanksgiving table centerpiece. The sky was blue and the air was crisp. The autumn colors were breathtaking. The situation just cried out for mugs of apple cider. We drove on until we found another roadside stand selling the basic ingredient. The following recipe will serve four to six. Double for a large gathering.

1 quart apple cider
3 cups cranberry juice

2 sticks cinnamon
3 cloves
¼ cup brown sugar

Put all ingredients in a coffee pot or deep pan. Heat until mixture bubbles. Serve steaming mugs and if desired a cinnamon stick for stirring. (Not bad served with doughnuts either.)

Bronze Punch

1 cup apricot nectar
1 can frozen pineapple juice

1 cup strong tea
1 cup water
1 quart ginger ale

Combine all ingredients except ginger ale and stir until well blended. Chill in the refrigerator until ready to serve. Add the ginger ale at the last minute. Serve over ice cubes.

Have a Cow

There are many cows to choose from: a *black* cow, a *purple* cow, a *white* cow or an *orange* cow. Make up your own cow. As a youngster at camp I was introduced to the cow family. Why the name cow was applied I do not know. I only know I became fascinated with "the cows" and we have been having a cow ever since.

2 scoops of vanilla ice cream
a carbonated drink

Put one scoop ice cream in a glass. Fill half full with the beverage you have chosen. Stir until blended. Add second scoop of ice cream and fill glass with the beverage. Use a straw and a spoon to devour every last drop.

For a black cow use root beer or coke

For a purple cow use grape soda

For a white cow use ginger ale or 7-Up

For an orange cow use orange crush

Orangeade

juice of 1 orange
2 tablespoons sugar

½ cup water
1 lemon slice

Squeeze orange and strain out seeds. Put in a glass with sugar and stir until sugar is dissolved. Add water. Pour into large glass with ice cubes and float lemon slice on top.

Variation: Use tangerines instead of oranges. A nice change of pace.

Pack the Stand-bys

Tea bags are packed easier than bulk teas. They are light weight and are easy to store. Some of our favorites are:

Constant Comment
Plantation Mint

Lemon Lift
Cinnamon Stick
Rose Garden

This gives a change to everyday tea and the variety makes the choice of which tea to serve fun and challenging.

Coffee
Decaffinated coffee

Café Mocha
Café Viennese
Café Capri

For still other taste tempters add whipping cream, ice cream, sprinkle of nutmeg, or a dash of liqueur.

A goodly number of small cans make an easy one person serving. Blend them or add other spices or flavorings.

grape juice
apple juice
pineapple juice

grapefruit juice
tomato juice
vegetable juice

Fresh lemon and lime juice perk up almost any fruit drink. You may want to take a supply of bottled juice for the time when you just may have run out of the real thing.

THE PERMANENT PANTRY

We feel that part of the pleasure of getting into the outdoors by means of a camper is that time may be saved, bad weather may be avoided and certain of the luxuries of modern refinements team together for greater enjoyment of leisure time.

Since we use and enjoy our camper regularly, we keep it in condition for travel on a moment's notice. In fact, our *return home* checklist includes checking the oil, tire pressure, fresh water supplies, toilet, gas, firewood and dozens of other small things which control our ability to use the camper often and get the most out of owning the unit.

One of the most important parts of that return home checklist is the immediate refurbishing of what we refer to as "The Permanent Pantry," a rather complete list of foodstuffs which are replenished as soon after using as possible. This broadens the versatility since we are reasonably well-prepared for an outing without much last minute preparation. The criteria for foods which go into the permanent pantry are simple but precise.

All foods must be storable in the unit for extended periods and not subject to spoilage. All foods are stored for space efficiency and they must not rattle. There is nothing more disconcerting than to put up with the monotonous sound of things rattling in cabinets.

190

We use scraps of polyurethane to wedge between rattling pans etc. We also use towels and carpet squares under or between other rattling items such as canned goods and the like. A dishwashing sponge in the oven prevents rattling of the racks and is also a good place to dry them out. Invent ways to prevent this problem. It will preserve the good nature of the driver.

Our list may differ from yours but these are the items we have available in the permanent pantry.

The Permanent Pantry

Beverages
   coffee
   tea
   cocoa
   canned soft drinks
   powdered drink mixes
   powdered milk
   canned fruit juices
   canned tomato juices

Cereals
   dry cereals
   cereals to be cooked
      oatmeal
      wheat & grain

Condiments
   vinegar
   Worcestershire sauce
   catsup
   mustard
   hot sauce

Meats
   canned:
      beef

   salmon
   tuna
   bacon
   Vienna sausages
   chipped beef
   crab
   shrimp
   lobster
   clams

Vegetables
   carrots
   peas
   beans
   potatoes
   tomatoes
   beets
   asparagus
   mushrooms

Fruits
   canned:
      apples
      pears
      pineapple
      peaches

apricots
berries
plums
cherries
dried:
   prunes
   raisins
   apples
   apricots

Staples
   sugar
   cornmeal
   masa
   flour
   spaghetti
   macaroni
   rice
   noodles
   biscuit and pancake mix
   popcorn

Seasonings, Spices & Herbs
   covered in section

Soups
   canned (various)
   packages (various dry)

Miscellaneous
   salad or cooking oil
   marshmallows
   dehydrated onions
   nuts
   jams and jellies
   peanut butter
   baking powder
   baking soda
   honey
   chili sauce
   syrups
   gravy mixes
   salad dressing mixes

SUBSTITUTIONS

Broth   canned broth, bouillon cubes, or consommé

Butter   margarine, or shortening (add ½ teaspoon per cup), for grilling sandwiches you may spread with mayonnaise instead of butter

Cream Cheese   cottage cheese blended with enough cream to make a smooth mixture

Chocolate (1 square unsweetened)   1 tablespoon shortening and 3 tablespoons cocoa

Flour (for thickening 2 cups liquid)   2 tablespoons flour, or 1 tablespoon arrowroot, or 1 tablespoon cornstarch, or

1 tablespoon flour plus 1 teaspoon quick-cooking tapioca

Herbs   1 tablespoon fresh or 1 teaspoon dried (use either)

Honey   molasses, corn syrup, or sorghum

Lemon   lime—bottled, canned or fresh

Lime   lemon—bottled, canned or fresh

Milk   instant dried milk, or evaporated milk using ½ cup evaporated milk and ½ cup water for each 1 cup milk

Buttermilk   1 cup milk and 1 tablespoon vinegar for each 1 cup buttermilk

Rice   white, brown, wild, or mixed

Baking Soda   baking powder

Sour Cream (1 cup)   1 cup heavy cream and 1 teaspoon lemon juice—or—1 cup cream style cottage cheese, 2 tablespoons milk, 1½ tablespoons lemon juice blended until smooth

Sugar   honey—use to taste in sweeting use slightly less in baking

Vegetable Oil   salad oil or olive oil

Whipped Cream   non-dairy toppings

Heavy Coffee Cream   mix dry milk with half the amount of water

THE LAST MINUTE LIST

If the permanent pantry is properly stocked, the "last minute list" is easily handled without delaying the start of the trip. These are *our* basics.

Meats
  bacon
  ground beef
  sausage
  sandwich meats

Vegetables
  lettuce
  celery
  tomatoes
  carrots
  choice of others

Dairy
- milk
- eggs
- cheese
- cottage cheese
- butter

Sundry
- canned biscuits
- refrigerator rolls
- onions
- mayonnaise
- coffee

Obviously, there are other, more perishable, last minute food items you may wish to take. Regardless of *how* the planning in advance for food on the go is done, the important thing is that it be done—systematically. A great deal of the fun can be instantly gone upon discovering that an essential food item is on a shelf at home.

INDEX

9594